CORPORATE DISCLOSURE
in the
BANKING INDUSTRY

CORPORATE DISCLOSURE
in the
BANKING INDUSTRY
Evidence from Nigeria

DAVID ISIAVWE, PH.D.

CORPORATE DISCLOSURE IN THE BANKING INDUSTRY
EVIDENCE FROM NIGERIA

iUniverse books may be ordered through booksellers or by contacting:

iUniverse
1663 Liberty Drive
Bloomington, IN 47403
www.iuniverse.com
1-800-Authors (1-800-288-4677)

ISBN: 978-1-5320-1426-0 (sc)
ISBN: 978-1-5320-1427-7 (e)

Library of Congress Control Number: 2017900254

Print information available on the last page.

iUniverse rev. date: 02/06/2017

CONTENTS

CHAPTER THREE

CHAPTER FOUR

CHAPTER FIVE

DISCUSSIONS, CONCLUSIONS AND RECOMMENDATIONS.... 77

LIST OF TABLES

DEDICATION

This book is dedicated first to God Almighty, the Lord and Creator of the entire universe. It is further dedicated to Afoke, Ufuoma, Ogaga, Fiona, Runo and Ogheneruona as well as the Information Security Society of Africa, Nigeria (ISSAN); Urhobo Social Club of Lagos and to every scholar who desires to gain further knowledge in the field of corporate governance and disclosure.

ACKNOWLEDGEMENTS

I wish to acknowledge the ever present help provided by Jehovah God through the years towards the achievement of this work and the significant contributions of the great men and women who have been associated directly and indirectly with me in my journey through life thus far.

I am particularly grateful to the visionary leader and founder of Igbinedion University Okada, His Excellency, Sir Chief Dr. Osawaru Igbinedion, CON; The Esama of Benin Kingdom who provided the enabling environment for this dream to become a reality as well as His Royal Majesty, Oghenekevwe Owin Kumane Eruvwedede III, (J.P) the Ovie of Evwreni Kingdom for the support and encouragement through the years. I am also grateful to Professor and Dr. (Mrs) Famous Izedonmi, who were used by the Spirit of God to water the seed of the doctoral programme that is the bedrock for this work. My special thanks also go to Professor Grace Alele Williams, Professor Abhulimen R. Anao, Professor Osayuki Oshodin, Professor Arinze E. Okoye, Professor Bernard E. Owumi, Professor Chinwumba A. Okafor and Dr. Augustine Enofe for their excellent support over the years. Furthermore, I will like to acknowledge the significant insights provided by Dr. Dickson Oriakhi, Dr. Eyesan Dabor, Dr. James. Ilaboya, Dr. Sule Omoye, Dr. Adesina Oladipupo, Dr. Ibrahim Ibn Shaibu, Dr. Okun Omokhudu, and Dr. Chijioke Mgbame.

My special thanks also go to Professor Eghosa Osaghae, the Vice-Chancellor, Igbinedion University, Professor Adeleke A. Ojo, Dean of Postgraduate School, Igbinedion University, Dr. Steve Ughulu, the Sub-Dean of Postgraduate School, Igbinedion University, Rev. Festus Osasere, the Secretary of Postgraduate School, Igbinedion University, Chief Dr. Raph

Adeghe, Dean, College of Business and Management Studies, Igbinedion University and Dr. Samson A. Adediran, the able and indefatigable Head of Department of Accounting, Igbinedion University, Okada, for the invaluable role they all played in actualizing this dream in my life.

Special thanks also go to all the great men and women who have assisted in one way or the other with this success story especially, in the early days when my scholastic ideas were still untested. They persevered through it all and saw the process of refinement that it went through. I am also eternally grateful to all who assisted with data extraction and analysis as well as the provision of logistics support over time. Some of the great men and women include Dr. Beshiru Sanusi, Dr. Mary Josiah, Dr. Betty Ali-Momoh, Dr. (Mrs) Toyin Afolabi, Dr. Kingsley Omimi-Ejoor Atu, Dr. Odion Oziegbe, Dr. Gbenga Ekundayo, Comrade Ileleji Phillip, Mr. Emmanuel Agu, Mr. Sunday Sule, Mr. Jude Aruomaghe, Mr. Emmanuel Okoebor, Ms. Josephine Omorodion, Mr. Segun Famoriyo, Ms. Ngozi Osuigwe, Mr. Friday Okpe, Dr. Francis Okoye, Mr. Boniface Asinobi, Mr. Abel Enechaziam, Mr. Oluwagbenga Adeoye, Mr. Oladapo Afikode, Mr. Tajudeen Akande and a host of others too numerous to mention. I sincerely appreciate you all.

Furthermore, I will like to thank the Management and Staff of UBA Plc, Union Bank of Nigeria Plc, Rainbow Specialist Medical Centre, The Information Security Society of Africa, Nigeria (ISSAN), The Institute of Chartered Accountants of Nigeria (ICAN), the Chartered Institute of Bankers of Nigeria (CIBN) and the Nigerian Stock Exchange (NSE) for their collaborative support and encouragement during the period of this endeavour.

My special thanks and appreciation also go to Chief (Dr) Kola Jamodu, OFR, Dr. Tony Elumelu, CON, Olorogun O'tega Emerhor, Mr. Ade Ayeyemi, the Late Dr. Harold George Osuagwu, Dr. Tony Iredia, Mr. Taukeme Koroye, Mr. Emeka Emuwa, Mrs. Oyinkansade Adewale, Mr. Kandolo Kasongo, Eng. Mansur Ahmed, Dr. Onikepo Akande CON (Mrs), Dr. Marcel Ojinka, Mr. Lucky Jayaratne, Mr. Matthew Akinlade, Alh. Musa Baba Bichi and Alh. Ibrahim Kwargana for mentoring and providing support and encouragement over the years. Further thanks and appreciation also go to Prof. Pat Donwa, Prof. P.A. Isenmila, Dr. Obi Anyaduba, Mr. Olufemi Adeyanju, Mr. Frank Omo-Amadasun KSJ,

Chief Brown Zimughan, Chief Abraham Odjighoro, Mr. Fatai Karim, Mr Femi Olaloku, Elder Emmanuel Nnorom, Mr. Nath Ude, Mr. Kushal Duneja, Mr. Dipo Fatokun, Mr. Osioke Ojior, Mr. John Anthony Olusoga, Prof. Segun Ajibola, Mr. Seye Awojobi, Mr. Usman Isiaka, Mr. Connor Crombie, Mr. Harold Groothedde, Mr. Tony Wagbafor, Mr. Obaro Osah, Dr. Theophilus Otuguor, Pastor Freeborn Ukpede, Mr. Kemi Balogun (SAN), Mr. Martin Etireri, Mr. Felix Ekpo, Barr. Olasupo Ati-John, Bishop Emmanuel Odjighoro, Dr. Tony Rapu, Mr. Victor Osadolor, Mr. Elias Igbinakenzua, Mr. Efe Akhigbe, Mr. Jim Obazee, Mr. Titus Osawe, Mr. Isaac Igbinojo, Mr. Felix Edosomwan J.P., Mr. Emmanuel Umukoro, Mr. Harris Osarenren, Mr. Tony Ezeani, Mr. Laja Sorunke, Mr. Udochi Nwaodu, Mr. Felix Igbinosa, Dr. Martin Ikpehai, Mrs Adedoyin Odunfa, Mr. Joseph Esenwa, Mr. Craig Rosewarne, Mr. Tunde Ekpekurede, Pastor Wale Adedokun, Chief Johnson M. Barovbe, Chief Simeon Ohwofa, Snr. Evang. Emmanuel Evue, Prof. Edward Emuveyan, Mr. Diamond Okotete, Eng. Godwin Onabedje, Prof. Ben Akpoyomare Oghojafor, Chief Austine Enajemo Isire, Chief Chris Umukoro of blessed memory, Mr. Francis Ewherido, all the great men of Urhobo Social Club Lagos (and a host of others too numerous to mention) for their love and friendship over the years. May the good Lord bless you all.

I will also like to express my deepest appreciation to all of my in-laws as well as my numerous brothers and sisters for their unalloyed demonstration of love over the years and for accommodating me in their space. My special thanks also go to my dear wife, Afoke, and our five children for branding me "the best daddy in the world" despite my obvious failings. Also, I will like to thank my parents, the late Chief and Mrs Samuel Eretchabor ISIAVWE, J.P; for bringing us up in the way of the Lord and giving me the chance to take up the daunting challenge of acquiring a doctorate degree. Finally, I give all the glory to Jehovah God for the grace to complete this book successfully.

PREFACE

This book is the end result of a study conducted to empirically investigate the determinants of corporate disclosure by banks in Nigeria. It is the second book of the Dr. Isiavwe series of publications on the dynamics of banking in Nigeria. The sample of banks reviewed consisted of nineteen out of the twenty one deposit money banks in Nigeria as at 31/12/2013. The other two banks had incomplete data.

An un-weighted dichotomous methodology was used in which the disclosure items were assigned a score of "1" if they were reported or a value of "0" if they were not reported. A disclosure index consisting of two hundred and nineteen (219) disclosure items was used to evaluate the content of the annual reports. Panel design was adopted for the study. Variables used in the model include Disclosure Index (DISINDEX) as the dependent variable while the independent variables include Firms' Size (TASSETS), Banks' age (AGE), Profitability (PAT), International Subsidiaries (INTSUB), Financial Expertise (FINEXP) and Board Independence (BOARDIND). The study used Descriptive Statistics, Correlation Analysis, pooled and panel regression analysis and other diagnostic tests like multicollinearity, heteroskedasticity and autocorrelation. The model was estimated with the aid of a computer software (E-views 8.0).

The study found that the major determinants of disclosure by banks in Nigeria are the size of bank, bank profitability, presence of international subsidiaries and preponderance of board members with financial expertise. These variables have a significant positive relationship with the disclosure index of banks. However, bank age and the presence of non-executive directors on the board had a positive impact but were not statistically significant in determining the disclosure posture of banks in Nigeria. The study concluded that big and profitable banks tend to disclose more information to stakeholders. Also, banks whose directors have a financial background are more likely to disclose more information. Furthermore, the presence of international subsidiaries expands the reporting scope of banks.

The study recommends that banks in Nigeria should be encouraged to grow their balance sheet and profitability for enhanced disclosure. The government should create an enabling environment while bank regulators should take innovative steps to reduce their operational costs. The Chartered Institute of Bankers in Nigeria (CIBN) should introduce a mandatory annual continuing educational requirement for bank directors.

This book will therefore be very useful to boards of directors of banks both in Nigeria as well as the international community. Also, bank regulators, lecturers and students in the departments of Banking and Finance, Accounting, Business Administration and allied courses will find this book a compelling read.

Furthermore, Accounting Practitioners, shareholders, external and internal auditors, investment analysts, stockbrokers, legislators and the general public will find this book quite useful. The unique disclosure index of 219 disclosure items will further aid and illuminate future research into banking disclosures in Nigeria.

ISIAVWE, T. David, Ph.D.
(FCA; CISSP, CGEIT, CISM, CISA; HCIB)

CHAPTER ONE

INTRODUCTION

1.1 Background

Corporate disclosure is critical to the functioning of an efficient capital market. Organizations usually provide disclosure through regulated financial reports including financial statements, footnotes, management discussion and analysis, and other regulatory filings. In addition, some firms engage in voluntary communication such as management forecasts, analysts' presentations and conference calls, press releases, internet sites, and other corporate reports (Healy and Palepu, 2001). Stakeholders therefore, rely on financial statements as presented by managements to make decisions. These range from investment decisions by both current and potential investors to financing decisions by creditors, governmental agencies, employees, investment analysts, rating agencies, etc. All of these stakeholders make critical decisions using the financial statements (Kam, 1990; Okoye, 1996; 2000).

The quality of decisions that investors can make is largely dependent on the quality of information available to them. This information can be classified into quantitative (financial) and qualitative (non-financial). However, financial information is of great significance as it requires a reasonable level of skill to interpret and use it. The published financial statements prepared by directors of limited liability companies in general and banks in particular remain the primary means of informing shareholders and other users about the financial performance, progress and position of the business (Glautier, Underdown & Morris, 2011).

However, the spate of corporate failures that occurred in the past two decades involving several banks and other corporate entities such as Abacus Merchant Bank, ABC Merchant Bank, Allied Bank of Nigeria Plc, Amicable Bank of Nigeria Ltd, Commerce Bank Ltd, Continental Merchant Bank Plc, Co-Operative and Commerce Bank, Credite Bank Nigeria Ltd, Group Merchant Bank Ltd, Nigeria Merchant Bank Ltd;, Pinnacle Commercial Bank Ltd, Peak Merchant Bank, Enron, WorldCom, Global Crossing, Adelphia Communications, HIH, Tyco, Vivendi, Royal Ahold and HealthSouth, together with a host of other company/bank failures worldwide, has further exacerbated the problem of relying on financial statements released by business organizations due to incomplete and inappropriate disclosure. Coupled with the perceived increase in the frequency of window dressed financial statements worldwide, all of this has had a negative and cumulative impact on the way informed opinion views financial reporting (International Federation of Accountants – [IFAC] 2003; Ogubunka, 2003).

Furthermore, IFAC (2003) reported that there has been great concern, in some cases approaching outrage, regarding the "fairness" of the operation of a market system where shareholders, employees in general, and pensioners have lost large sums, while those running companies and perceived by members of the public to be responsible for those losses have enriched themselves even though their businesses collapsed. The cumulative impact of these high profile cases has led to a steady loss in the credibility of financial statements and of the participants involved with producing and reporting on them. Indeed, the 1980s and 1990s are littered with examples of corporate failure generally associated with dubious reporting coupled with non-adherence to the principles of corporate governance. In the U.K for instance, these include names such as Maxwell, BCCI, Polly Peck and Barings. France has Credit Lyonnais; Germany adds Metalgesellschaft and Schneider; Australia provides AWA, Bond, Spedley Securities, and Tricontinental; Canada adds Canadian Commercial Bank, Castor Holdings and Roman Corporation; Japan has Yamaichi; and the U.S. has the many examples from the savings and loan industry as well as cases such as Cendant, Sunbeam, Waste Management,

Wedtech, and ZZZZ Best. The East Asian financial crisis in the second half of 1997 also raised questions about the reliability of financial statements and about the role of the large international accounting firms in reporting on them (IFAC, 2003).

In Nigeria, we have also had our share of failed corporations as well as celebrated cases of inappropriate financial reporting involving companies like Union Dicon Salt, Lever Brothers (Now Unilever Plc), Cadbury Nig Plc and several Banks (Randle, 2012 & Sambo, 2011). This book therefore is based on a research that was conducted on the banking industry in the year 2015. It is the second of the Dr. Isiavwe series of publications on the Dynamics of Banking in Nigeria and focuses on the determinants of corporate disclosure in the banking industry in Nigeria.

1.2 Statement of the Research Problem

Corporate governance and disclosure are critical to the efficient operations of modern financial markets. This is particularly relevant in capitalist environments where there is a clear dichotomy between the owners of a business (the shareholders) and the managers. This situation, as exemplified by the agency relationship between the owners and managers, must be continuously managed in order to have a harmonious financial system with enhanced accountability and transparency, reduced costs and utmost efficiency (Amihud & Mendelson, 1986; Cadbury Committee, 1992; Glosten & Milgrom, 1985; and Merton, 1987). There is a general widespread suspicion of the huge figures disclosed as profits by financial institutions in Nigeria especially given the fact that over the years, many of those institutions have failed due to inappropriate reporting and mismanagement coupled with other factors.

Therefore, given the fact that banking system stability is fundamental to the stability, growth and development of the general economy (Central Bank of Nigeria, 2013), it is imperative that the disclosure practices by banks in Nigeria are comparable with what obtains in other more advanced and developed markets. The importance of this is further heightened by the fact that any negative development that significantly hampers the growth and stability of banks in Nigeria has a spillover effect not only on the Nigerian economy but also on the economies of other neighboring countries in the West African Sub-Region (International Monetary Fund – [IMF], 2013). This is even more relevant now that Nigeria is the biggest economy in Africa based on the rebasing of its GDP to $510 Billion (Ainofenokhai, 2014; Atuanya & Augie, 2014). It is critical, therefore, to ensure that all regulatory bodies and bank operators take steps to assure the investing and depositing public of the safety of their funds and investments.

Furthermore, there is a paucity of studies in Nigeria that highlight the major determinants of disclosure by deposit money banks that operate in Nigeria. Also, given the fact that the Nigerian banking environment reflects the general state of underdevelopment of the economy, it is not clear how much voluntary disclosure is being done by Nigerian banks and how well banks comply with the mandatory items of disclosure. Regulators like The Securities and Exchange Commission (SEC), The Central Bank of Nigeria (CBN), Corporate Affairs Commission (CAC), The Financial Reporting Council (FRC) and others are increasingly demanding greater disclosures from banks and listed companies to ensure that the financial institutions do not become victims of the same predisposing factors that were responsible for the collapse of the global financial system (Ogujiuba & Obiechina, 2011).

This study was thus carried out to critically evaluate the level of disclosure by banks in their annual reports and by implication, the key factors that determine the posture of corporate disclosure by bank operators in the Nigerian environment. This is based on the fundamental and highly disturbing problem of bank distress in Nigeria given the many bank failures which have been recorded in the history of banking in Nigeria which were attributable to inappropriate disclosure and poor management (Ogubunka, 2003). Indeed, the incidence of bank failures was so rampant that bank distress became a common lexicon in Nigeria (Ogubunka, 2003).

1.3 Objectives of the Study

The primary objective of this study was to evaluate the determinants of corporate disclosure by bank operators in Nigeria with a special focus on financial statement disclosure. The specific objectives are to:

1. establish if the size of banks has any significant impact on corporate disclosure.
2. ascertain if the age of banks has any significant impact on corporate disclosure in their annual report.
3. determine the impact of the level of bank profitability on corporate disclosure by banks.
4. determine if board members with financial expertise have a significant influence on disclosure of information in the annual report of Nigerian banks.
5. ascertain if banks with international subsidiaries disclose more information than banks that only have local presence.
6. establish if the composition of the board has any significant impact on corporate disclosure.

1.4 Relevant Research Questions

From the above, this study can be described as a rigorous scholastic attempt to answer the fundamental questions that are listed below.

1. What is the relationship between the size of a bank and its disclosure posture?
2. What is the relationship between the age of a bank and its disclosure posture?
3. Is there any relationship between the profitability of a bank and its disclosure posture?
4. What is the relationship between the number of board members with financial expertise and the disclosure of information in the annual report?
5. What impact do international subsidiaries of banks have on the disclosure practices of the parent companies?
6. Does the composition of the board of a bank affect its disclosure of information?

1.5 Research Hypotheses

Based on the specific objectives to be achieved in this study, the following hypotheses which are stated in null form were tested.

- Ho1. There is no relationship between the total assets and the level of disclosure of the banks in Nigeria.
- Ho2. The age of banks operating in Nigeria has no significant impact on the level of disclosure in their annual reports.
- Ho3. The performance of banks operating in Nigeria has no significant impact on the level of disclosure in their annual reports.
- Ho4. Board members with financial expertise in Nigerian banks have no significant influence on disclosure of information in the annual reports.
- Ho5. Banks with international subsidiaries whose headquarters are based in Nigeria do not disclose more information than banks with only local branches.
- Ho6. There is no relationship between the composition of the board of Nigerian banks and the level of disclosure.

1.6 The Scope of the Study

The subject matter of this study was restricted to financial statement disclosure in the Nigerian banking industry. In order to achieve the set objectives of the study, data covering the years 2005 to 2013 were collected and analyzed for all the twenty one (21) deposit money banks licensed by the Central Bank of Nigeria. The population of the study therefore, consists of all 21 banks licensed to operate as Deposit Money Banks (DMBs) in Nigeria as at December, 31 2013 (CBN, 2014). This was due to the need to ensure that a holistic view of disclosure was obtained for all bank operators in Nigeria with a view to ascertaining the major determinants of disclosure in the banking Industry.

1.7 Significance of the Study

Inappropriate disclosure in financial statements is a worrisome development in all financial markets across the world and must be tackled as a matter of urgency to ensure that the failing credibility of financial statements is halted across the entire value chain of the financial report preparation, examination and dissemination process. Therefore, the core determinants of corporate disclosure by banks in Nigeria must be evaluated critically in order to ensure that there is full appreciation of the factors that determine what banks disclose in Nigeria. This is therefore the gap that this study set out to fill.

Indeed, the problem of inappropriate disclosure in financial statements is further exacerbated by the fact that there is a paucity of empirical studies in developing countries especially in the area of credibility of financial reports in relation to corporate disclosure deficiencies (Needles, 1997; Okeahalam & Akinboade, 2003). This is because, though there are several studies in this field, a significant proportion thereof focuses on developed economies of the world to the detriment of African economies. There is also no comprehensive disclosure index in Nigeria for the purpose of evaluating the key drivers of disclosure in Nigeria.

This study, therefore empirically evaluated the extent of disclosure by banks in Nigeria with a view to ascertaining the major determinants of disclosure by the key operators in the banking industry in the country. All banks in the country, including those that are listed on the Nigerian Stock Exchange as well as non listed banks, were covered in the study. Specific areas of focus include a review of the corporate profile of the banks, financial information published in the annual reports coupled with periodic financial information and financial highlights, corporate governance, management structure and board composition.

This study is particularly relevant as it addressed all the elements of disclosure that are applicable to the banking industry in Nigeria. For this purpose, a disclosure index of two hundred and nineteen (219) elements specifically tailored to the Nigerian banking industry was designed and used in the study. The disclosure index took into cognizance all relevant disclosure requirements in Nigeria as well as international best practices.

Overall, this research work will be beneficial to the following interest groups.

Regulators

The regulatory authorities will find the results of this study useful in the conduct of their oversight functions over the banks as it will afford them the opportunity of appreciating from a fairly rigorous research perspective, the major drivers of corporate disclosure in the banking industry. In addition, the results of this study will assist in the formulation of policies by the regulators to improve the overall disclosure posture of banks and by extension the health and safety of the entire banking system.

Bank Operators and Management

This study is also significant to bank operators, their boards and executive management teams who will find the results invaluable as the study will serve as a mirror through which they can independently and objectively assess their disclosure posture vis-à-vis their peers in the industry. The study will also enable them to take necessary remedial action to improve on their overall disclosure posture.

Accounting Practitioners and Academicians

It is expected that the result of this research will be beneficial to both accounting practitioners and academicians. This is primarily because they are responsible for collating the information that forms the bedrock of the disclosure posture of banks. Whereas researchers will gain greater analytical clarity in this subject area, practitioners, on the other hand, will gain insights into the main drivers of disclosure by banks.

Investors and Shareholders

Investors and shareholders will undoubtedly benefit from this study as it will provide an opportunity for them to better understand the dynamics of the banks especially in the area of corporate disclosure. It will also enable them to take crucial investment decisions based on this enhanced knowledge. Indeed, there is no doubt that the results of this research will serve as a veritable input in determining the outlook of investors as they will be better informed about the disclosure posture of banks in Nigeria vis-à-vis their counterparts in other parts of the world.

External and Internal Auditors of Banks

It is believed also that external auditors will find this study useful as they will be able to incorporate the results in the determination of the sample size of their audits in the different banks. It will also serve to improve the conduct of their work in the field and the overall disclosure posture of banks in the industry will be enhanced thereby. This also applies to all internal auditors in banks as it will facilitate and strengthen the process of applying the risk based methodology in their sample selection and testing based on the areas where there is need for improvement in their respective organizations.

Other groups of persons who will benefit from the results of this study include investment analysts, research students, stock brokers, legislators and the public at large.

1.8 Limitations of the Study

Given the fairly nascent state of development of research in Africa generally (Nigeria inclusive), a myriad of problems typically bedevil any research of this nature. In this regard therefore, the limitations of this study include the following:

1. Inadequate Reliable Data.

The data used for this study spans a period of nine years. There was no guarantee that the required data could be obtained in a reliable and consistent form given the fact that there have been significant developments in the banking industry which have impacted on the capacity of several banks to operate during the period under review. There is also the possibility that some of the data obtained from different sources might be conflicting or inconsistent (Osazee and Izedonmi, 2008).

2. Bureaucratic Secrecy.

In Nigeria (as in most developing countries), it is generally believed that corporate information and data are high level secrets that cannot be divulged to researchers. This is in spite of the fact that a great deal of the information should normally be published in the public domain to assist both researchers and interested stakeholders to make relevant decisions. The difficulty experienced in obtaining relevant information is therefore regarded as one of the limitations of this study.

3. Financial Inclusion in the Nigerian Banking Industry

In Nigeria, about 65 per cent of the population are excluded from the formal banking industry (Ajakaiye and Olowookere, 2013; Digital Africa, 2013 and World Bank, 2012). Therefore, the data that was collected and analyzed in this study is limited to the transactions that were done by the 35 per cent of the Nigerian population. Under normal circumstances, data relating to the full population ought to be collected and analyzed in the study. This is therefore regarded as a limitation in this study.

1.9 Definition of Key Terms

In order to assure profound clarity and specificity of key terms used in this study, the following definitions are hereby provided:

Agency Relationship
This is the relationship that exists between two parties – a principal and his or her agent and the entire spectrum of actions and decisions which are taken by the agent while contractually bound to the principal (Kiel and Nicholson, 2003).

Banking Business.
The Banks and other Financial Institutions Act {BOFIA (2004)} defines banking business as the business of receiving deposits or current account, savings account or other similar account, paying or collecting cheques drawn by or paid in by customers; provision of finance or such other business as the Governor of the Central Bank may so designate.

Deposit:
BOFIA (2004) also defines the term "deposit" as money lodged with any person whether or not for the purpose of any interest or dividend and whether or not such money is repayable upon demand upon a given period of notice or upon a fixed date.

Banking Industry
This refers to the collection of individuals, companies and institutions that engage in banking business in accordance with the extant laws of the country. It is important to note that the banking industry in Nigeria (as in most countries of the world) is heavily regulated.

Board of Directors
Investopedia (2013) defines a board of directors as a group of individuals who are elected to act as representatives of the shareholders to establish corporate management related policies and to make decisions on major company issues. Such issues include the hiring/firing of executives, dividend policies, options policies and executive compensation. Every public company must have a board of directors.

Central Bank of Nigeria (CBN)
The CBN is defined as the apex regulatory authority of the financial system in Nigeria. It was established by the Central Bank of Nigeria Act of 1958 and commenced operations on 1st July 1959. Among its primary functions, the Bank promotes monetary stability and a sound financial system, and acts as a banker and financial advisor to the Federal Government, as well as being a banker of last resort to all other banks in the country.

Corporate Governance
Corporate governance can be defined as the system by which companies are directed and controlled by the executive management, the board and shareholders. Whereas the board of directors are responsible for the governance and supervision of the company, shareholders appoint the directors and the auditors to satisfy themselves that an appropriate governance structure is in place.

Disclosure

This refers to the release of information about the activities of a company (Gernon and Meek, 2001). It has the capacity to mitigate resource misallocation on the capital market by reducing information asymmetries between insiders and investors and the associated cost of capital.

CHAPTER TWO

LITERATURE REVIEW

2.1. Introduction

This chapter discusses literature relating to corporate disclosure and corporate governance in Nigerian banking industry. The chapter begins with a review of the concepts of corporate disclosure and corporate governance, and of the independent variables as well as the conceptual framework of this study. This is in turn followed by a review of the theoretical framework, prior studies, the history of banking, and the philosophy and elements of banking reforms.

2.2. Corporate Disclosure

Investopedia (2013) defined disclosure as the act of releasing all relevant information pertaining to a company that may influence an investment decision. For companies that operate in market driven environments where the stock market is regarded as a principal provider of finance for business, full disclosure is critical as the various shareholders and stakeholders require that all material information relating to the performance of the business be provided to aid decision making (Gernon & Meek, 2001). Full disclosure is thus one of the fundamental requirements for listing on all the major stock exchanges in the world (Investopedia, 2013).

Adina and Ion (2008) citing Gibbins, Richardson and Waterhouse (1992) opined that organizations may disclose information to support the efficiency of exchange and production. In addition, they may also disclose information to establish their compliance with the social values reflected in regulations and informal norms. They further went on to state that companies have at their disposal two kinds of publishing variants through which they can diminish the informational asymmetry of their stakeholders. These are compulsory and voluntary disclosure. In their view, compulsory disclosure is fundamental to the accounting reporting process as all eligible business organizations must satisfy the legal requirements of full disclosure.

DisclosureNet (2012) outlined the various types of information that can be obtained from corporate filings to include industry awareness, competitive intelligence, strategic decision making, risk management and best practices. Uyar and Kilic (2012), on the other hand, introduced the concept of "Forward-looking" information disclosure which refers to providing information which enables stakeholders to evaluate the future performance of a company. Citing Aljifri and Hussainey (2007) they opined that such forward-looking disclosure might involve both financial forecasts such as next year's earnings, expected revenues and anticipated cash flows and non-financial information such as risks and uncertainties that are likely to affect the performance of the firm. In their view, disclosing forward-looking information reduces information asymmetry between firms and stakeholders thus permitting stakeholders to make healthier decisions about companies. This is in contra distinction to backward-looking information which is largely provided by financial statements and narrative sections of the annual reports.

2.2 Corporate Governance and Disclosure

Healy and Palepu (2001) posited that financial reporting and disclosure are potentially important means for managements to communicate firms' performance and governance to outside investors. There is no doubt that quality financial accounting data enhances efficiency by enabling managers and investors to identify value creation opportunities with less error. In the views of Bushman and Smith, (2003) this in turn leads to more accurate allocation of capital to highest valued uses. Furthermore, it is widely believed that the credibility of management disclosures is enhanced by regulators, standard setters, auditors and other capital market intermediaries (Healy & Palepu, 2001). There is however, no empirical research evidence to support this perception. On the contrary, there is evidence that investors view voluntary disclosures such as management forecasts as credible information (Heidhues & Patel, 2010).

Turrent (2012) stated that in recent years there has been increased public interest in corporate transparency which is reflected in the issuance of new regulations in various countries. This is essentially to address the issue of the failing credibility of financial statements given the fairly scandalous and almost catastrophic financial meltdown experienced globally. In 1991, the American Institute of Certified Public Accountants (AICPA) established the Special Committee on Financial Disclosure in order to systematize the corporate information provided to stakeholders (AICPA, 1994). In 2002, the IFAC issued a document to ensure the consistency and comparability of information disclosed on the Internet to consider the type and format of information, the security and integrity of data, contacts and the use of different languages. In Spain, the Transparency Law was passed and a unified code of corporate transparency established in 2003. These were viewed as essential elements of good governance. In Mexico, the principles of transparency were addressed in the Stock Market Law and the Regulation for Issuers of 2006 taking into account The Organization for Economic Cooperation and Development (OECD) principles (Turrent, 2012).

In Nigeria, the Securities and Exchange Commission (SEC) issued the Code of Corporate Governance for quoted companies in 2011 whereas the Central Bank of Nigeria (CBN) had previously issued a Code of Corporate Governance for banks and financial Institutions in 2006. All of these efforts are geared towards ensuring that corporate disclosure and financial reporting are performed in accordance with best practices and to improve the level of credibility of financial reporting. Gray, Meek and Roberts (1995) were of the view that disclosure essentially reduces information asymmetry and uncertainty as stakeholders are able to ascertain the story behind the figures from the information provided. This eventually prevents market failure while at the same time it increases market liquidity.

Ştefănescu (2012) citing Lev (1992) stated that previous studies have shown that mandatory disclosure rules ensure equal access to basic information and help firms to communicate with their investors. This however, does not completely eliminate the "Agency" problem as management still has the upper hand regarding access to and control over corporate information. Without any doubt, constant communication through corporate disclosure is a very important aspect of corporate governance in the sense that a meaningful and adequate disclosure generally facilitates the corporate governance process in organizations (Bhasin, 2010). It is instructive to note that companies generally make voluntary disclosure a signaling tool to the external world and the content of such voluntary disclosure varies from one company to another (Collett & Hrasky 2005). It is further instructive to note that the subject of corporate governance is deeply rooted in the agency theory which is concerned with the relationship that exists between two parties – a principal and his or her agent and the entire spectrum of actions and decisions which are taken by the agent while contractually bound to the principal (Kiel & Nicholson, 2003). Citing Fama and Jensen (1983), Kiel and Nicholson (2003) further stated that the agency theory is primarily concerned with aligning the interests of owners with the managers' and this is based on the premise that there is an inherent conflict between the interests of a firm's owners and its management.

2.3 Measurement of Variables

This section presents a concise evaluation of the independent variables used in this study. They include bank size, age, profitability, financial expertise, presence of international subsidiaries and board independence.

2.3.1 Bank Size

In Nigeria, banks have been broadly classified into tiers depending on their size (CBN 2013). The size of a bank, therefore, could be related to the extent of disclosure in its annual report to shareholders and the investing public. Hossain (2008), for instance, found out that there is a significant correlation between firms' size and the extent of disclosure. Also, Singhvi and Desai (1971) adduced several reasons for this observation. These range from the fact that big banks communicate with a larger audience than smaller banks so they tend to disclose more information. In addition, the financial burden of collating and disclosing information is higher on smaller firms than larger ones thereby constricting the level of information gathering and dissemination by the smaller firms. Finally, smaller firms harbour the fear that too much disclosure could hamper their competitive position. This view agrees with the findings of Enofe and Isiavwe (2012) who found a significant linear relationship between firms' size as exemplified by total assets and the level of disclosure by banks. Therefore, the larger the bank, the higher the tendency of the bank to disclose more information in its annual reports. The positive and significant association between bank size and disclosure is consistent with prior findings by Al-Shammari, (2005), Barako, (2007) and Lan, Wang and Zhang (2013). However, the result contradicts Glaum and Street (2003), who found a negative association that is not significantly related to disclosure.

2.3.2 Age

As companies grow, it is expected that they will master their processes better, manage their cost of operations more effectively and develop a heritage over time. All of this should influence the level of disclosure, both mandatory and voluntary, by the companies. Hossain (2008) citing Owusu- Ansah (1998) highlighted three factors that contribute to this phenomenon. The first is that younger companies may suffer stiff competition that could hamper their ability to disclose information readily. Secondly, the cost burden on younger companies is significant in relation to their scale of operation. Thirdly, the younger companies do not have a track record comparable to that of the older companies. This study, therefore, sets out to determine the relationship between the age of banks and the extent of disclosure.

2.3.3 Profitability

Enofe and Isiavwe (2012) reported a strong positive relationship between banks' profitability and disclosure of information. This result also agrees with prior empirical studies such as Owusu-Ansah's (1998) and signaling theory which assert that companies use their financial statement as a signaling tool to express their expectations and intentions. According to

Singhvi and Desai (1971), the corporation may disclose more information when its profitability is above industry average in order to inform the shareholders and other stakeholders about the corporation's strong position to survive. This is also consistent with the findings of Hossain (2008) who reported a positive correlation between profitability and disclosure.

Karim and Ahmed (2005) also reported that corporate profitability affects disclosure in many ways. Citing Adelberg (1979), they posited that studies on the understandability of financial statement messages found that narrative disclosures in corporate annual reports are deliberately made complex to communicate bad news and made more lucid and easily understandable to communicate good news. They further stated that companies are likely to feel more comfortable when disclosing favourable rather than unfavourable information, because one of the objectives of information disclosure is to make share prices higher than expected profits. This tends to be good news for investors and other corporate stakeholders unless the company is a regulated utility. This position however contradicts the findings of Mendes-Da-Silva and Christensen (2004) who carried out a cross sectional study of 291 Brazilian companies on the determinants of voluntary disclosure of financial information on the internet and found higher levels of voluntary financial information disclosure by poorly performing companies.

2.3.4 Financial Expertise

The board composition of an organization which is typically a reflection of its ownership diffusion is a variable used to measure a firm's governance mechanism (Lan, Wang & Zhang {2013}). These authors posited that the more diffused the ownership of the organization, the better able its owners are to monitor managerial behaviour and thus require greater information disclosure. They reported that this position agrees with that of Alsaeed (2006) who found a positive relationship between the extent of voluntary disclosure and the ownership diffusion in Saudi Arabian companies whereas Haniffa and Cooke (2002), in contrast, showed that the level of disclosure among Malaysian companies is inversely related to their ownership diffusion level. They concluded that many other empirical studies have failed to find a statistically significant relationship.

Enofe and Isiavwe (2012) however reported that the size of the board with financial expertise has a significant influence on the disclosure of information in the annual report. This is expectedly so as a board that is comprised of persons who are learned in financial matters will be expected to bring to bear their financial expertise on the management of the banks that they oversee. This study was, therefore, conducted to ascertain the relationship between the presence of persons with financial expertise on the boards of Nigerian banks and the disclosure posture of the banks.

2.3.5 Presence of International Subsidiaries

Banks with international subsidiaries typically operate across different geographies and cultures with varying disclosure requirements. They are, therefore, likely to have a well built information system that can enable them to track all necessary and essential accounting information for internal and external purposes. It is expected that this will enable them to disclose accounting information more than their smaller counterparts. This position however, contradicts the position of Hossain (2008) who found no significant relationship between disclosure and the international subsidiaries of banks operating in India. The position however, agrees with the findings of Raffournier (1995) who studied the extent of disclosure in the annual reports of Swiss listed companies and discovered that size and internationality play a major role in the disclosure policy of large firms as internationally diversified companies tend to disclose information more than small purely domestic enterprises.

2.3.6 Board Independence

Board independence, as exemplified by the presence of non-executive directors on the board, is a critical factor to consider in determining the extent of disclosure on the annual reports and corporate governance by banks operating in Nigeria. Adeyemi and Fagbemi (2010), for instance, found that ownership by non-executive directors has the possibility of increasing the quality of auditing in Nigerian companies and by extension, their level of corporate governance and extent of disclosure. This is borne out of the overall influence that the non-executive directors are expected to have on the companies that they oversee.

Lan, Wang and Zhang (2013) posited that the proportion of non-executive directors on the board is an excellent measure of corporate governance or monitoring capability. In their view, non-executive directors are less aligned with management and are therefore more inclined to encourage firms to disclose a larger amount of information to outside investors. They confirmed that this position is in line with the findings of Jaggi and Low (2000) who found empirical evidence to show that the proportion of independent directors has a positive influence on disclosure in China.

2.4 Conceptual Framework

Corporate governance has indeed gained global prominence in recent years as there has been a growing recognition of the importance of effective corporate governance in ensuring sound financial reporting and disclosure. Furthermore, effective corporate governance ensures credible accounting and high quality financial reporting which provide the transparency of information that enables users like shareholders and investors to make informed decisions (Muhamad, Shahimi, Yahya, & Mahzan, 2009). There is the need therefore, to strengthen corporate governance practices and standards in companies that operate in Nigeria and across the world at large. Specifically, there is a compelling need to ensure that corporate governance practices in the banking industry in Nigeria are comparable to what obtains in other jurisdictions across the world given the highly sensitive role that banks play in the economy (The World Bank, 2012).

According to Deloitte (2013), the OECD defined corporate governance as procedures and processes according to which an organization is directed and controlled. The corporate governance structure outlines the specific distribution of rights and responsibilities among the different participants in the organization – such as the board, managers, shareholders and other stakeholders – and lays down the rules and procedures for decision-making which guide the activities of the organization.

Deloitte (2013) further outlined the definition of corporate governance by The Financial Times as how a company is managed in terms of the institutional systems and protocols meant to ensure accountability and sound ethics within the company. The concept encompasses a wide variety of issues, including the disclosure of information to shareholders and board members, the remuneration of senior executives, potential conflicts of interest among managers and directors, and supervisory structures.

Deloitte (2013) also cited the definition of corporate governance provided by the Cadbury Committee (1992) as the system by which companies are directed and controlled. The boards of directors are responsible for the governance and supervision of their companies. The shareholders' role in governance is to appoint the directors and the auditors to satisfy themselves that an appropriate governance structure is in place. The responsibilities of the board include setting the company's strategic aims, providing the leadership to put them into effect, supervising the management of the business and reporting to shareholders on their stewardship efforts of the company. The board's actions are subject to laws, regulations and the shareholders in general meetings.

It is instructive to note that there is a very close link between corporate governance and board effectiveness (Dabor & Adeyemi, 2009; Enofe & Isiavwe, 2012). In the view of Rezaee (2009), there are seven essential functions of corporate governance in any given organization. These can be enumerated as follows: oversight function, managerial function, compliance function, internal audit function, advisory function, external audit and monitoring functions.

Other definitions were provided by Baker and Anderson (2010) who were of the view that corporate governance refers to the way in which a business organization is directed, administered, and controlled. They also opined that corporate governance concerns the relationships among the various internal and external stakeholders involved as well as the governance processes designed to help a corporation achieve its goals.

McRitchie (2013), on the other hand, stated that the corporate governance framework of an organization usually depends on the legal, regulatory, institutional and ethical environment of the community. Citing Goergen (2012), he further stated that corporate governance deals with the conflicts of interests between the providers of finance and the managers; the shareholders and the stakeholders; different types of shareholders (mainly the large shareholder and the minority shareholders); and the prevention or mitigation of these conflicts of interests.

2.4.1 The Banking Industry in Nigeria

Ridwan (2011) posited that the evolution of banking in Nigeria pre-dates the nation's independence as it began with the activities of Elder Dempster and Company Limited of Liverpool, United Kingdom in 1892. This led to the establishment of the first bank in Nigeria which is the African Banking Corporation in 1892 (The Library of Congress Country Studies; CIA World Fact Book, 1991; Prani, 2005). According to Ridwan (2011), other notable organizations at that time included the Nigerian Mercantile Bank Limited, Nigerian Farmers and Commercial Bank Limited, British and French Bank (which transformed to UBA Plc otherwise known as Africa's Global Bank) up to the era of the Agbonmagbe Bank in 1945 which later transformed to WEMA Bank Plc and African Continental Bank (ACB) now defunct. The Library of Congress Country Studies and CIA World Fact book (1991) stated that no banking legislation existed until 1952 at which point Nigeria had three foreign banks (the Bank of British West Africa, Barclays Bank, and the British and French Bank) and two indigenous banks (the National Bank of Nigeria and the African Continental Bank) with a collective total of forty branches.

Unfortunately, most of the banks which had operated in Nigeria prior to independence were plagued by a myriad of problems including poor capitalization, incompetent management, stiff competition from better capitalized and efficiently run foreign competitors and the recession of the 1930s (Ridwan, 2011). Furthermore, there was no regulatory framework in those early days to regulate and supervise the activities of banks, thus the period between 1929 and1952 can be described as the era of laissez-faire in banking in Nigeria otherwise known as the era of "free" banking (Ridwan, 2011). However, the period from 1952 to 1959 saw the emergence of legislation and banking regulation with the enactment of the Banking Ordinance of 1952 and the establishment of The Central Bank of Nigeria.

The role of The Central Bank of Nigeria was to establish the Nigerian currency, control and regulate the banking system, serve as a banker to other banks in Nigeria, and carry out the government's economic policy in the monetary field. This policy included (but is not limited to) control of bank credit growth, credit distribution by sector, cash reserve requirements for commercial banks, discount rates - interest rates The Central Bank charged commercial and merchant banks - and the ratio of banks' long-term assets to deposits (The Library of Congress Country Studies; CIA World Fact book, 1991).

In the view of Ridwan (2011), this laid the foundation for the coordination and regulation of banking activities in Nigeria. Furthermore, the banking industry witnessed several negative developments over the course of time that led to the eventual amendments of the extant legislation to improve the overall regulatory environment of the banking industry. For instance, the 1969 Banking Act was enacted to correct the perceived weaknesses in the banking system and restore public confidence in the sector. Also, The Nigerian Deposit Insurance Corporation (NDIC) was established in 1988 to provide support for the CBN in managing the affairs of banks in the country. In 1991, the Banking and Other Financial institutions Act was proclaimed to replace both The Central Bank of Nigeria Act of 1958 and Banking Act of 1969 in order to further strengthen the powers of the CBN. This was also followed by a more recent amendment in 2007 which emphasizes monetary and price stability in the financial system (Ridwan, 2011).

It is instructive to note that the banking industry segment of the Nigerian financial system which includes the licensed deposit money banks, discount houses, finance companies, Bureaux De Change, primary mortgage institutions and microfinance banks have transformed over the years to assume the level of sophistication comparable to other emerging economies (Ridwan, 2011). Such areas of sophistication include new business models in terms of expansion and product offerings, innovation in electronic banking especially with the advent of the world wide web, massive deployment of information technology resources, regulation and supervision. It must be noted however, that the primary role of any banking system in any economy is financial intermediation. This involves the whole gamut of activities that support the transfer of financial resources from surplus saving units (SSUs) to deficit saving units (DSUs). The objective is to achieve a steady, progressive and balanced economic growth as well as long term economic development.

In 1973, the three largest commercial banks held about one-third of total bank deposits in the system. The Federal Government then undertook to acquire a 40-percent equity ownership of the three largest foreign banks. In 1976, under the second Nigerian Enterprises Promotion

Decree requiring 60-percent indigenous holdings, the Federal Government acquired an additional 20-percent holding in the three largest foreign banks and 60-percent ownership in the other foreign banks. Yet indigenization did not change the management, control, and lending orientation towards international trade, particularly of foreign companies and the Nigerian subsidiaries of foreign banks (The Library of Congress Country Studies; CIA World Fact Book, 1991; Prani, 2005).

It is further important to note that at the end of 1988, the banking system consisted of The Central Bank of Nigeria, forty-two commercial and twenty four merchant banks. This is a significant increase over the data for 1986. Merchant banks were allowed to open checking accounts for corporations only and could not accept deposits below N50,000.00. This is primarily due to the fact that the merchant banks engaged in wholesale banking in contra distinction to the commercial banks which engaged primarily in retail banking. Furthermore, both commercial and merchant banks together had 1,500 branches in 1988, up from 1,000 in 1984. During the year 1990, the government invested N503 million in establishing community banks to encourage community development associations, cooperative societies, farmers' groups, patriotic unions, trade groups, and other local organizations, especially in the rural areas to further stimulate financial inclusion and eventual all round development (The Library of Congress Country Studies; CIA World Fact book, 1991, Prani, 2005).

Ogujiuba and Obiechina (2011), citing Sylvanus and Abayomi (2001), stated that for more than two decades after independence, the Nigerian financial system was repressed. This was clearly demonstrated by ceilings on interest rates and credit expansion, selective credit policies, high reserve requirements, and restrictions on entry into the banking industry. In their view, this situation inhibited the functioning of the financial system and especially, constrained its ability to mobilize savings and facilitate productive investments. The banking industry, therefore, has witnessed significant reforms over time and hard choices have had to be made by the regulators and key stakeholders (Sanusi, 2012). Sanusi further opined that the financial system is more than just institutions that facilitate payments and extend credit. It encompasses all functions that direct real resources to their ultimate user. In his view, it is the central nervous system of a market economy and contains a number of separate, yet co-dependent components (like banks, insurance companies, the financial markets and the infrastructural component), all of which are essential to its effective and efficient functioning.

It is instructive to note that banks need payments systems infrastructure to exchange secure claims and markets in which to hedge the risks arising from their intermediation activities. The banking system, therefore, functions more efficiently and effectively when there is a robust and efficient payments systems infrastructure (Sanusi, 2012). Furthermore, the concern to ensure a sound banking system by The Central Bank is underscored by the critical role of banks in national economic development as banks generally mobilize savings for investment purposes which further generate growth and employment for the teaming mass of the people (World Bank, 2012).

The real sector, on the other hand, which is the productive sector of the economy relies heavily on the banking industry for credit. Furthermore, government raises funds through the banking system to finance its developmental programmes and strategic objectives. Based on these strategic roles of the banking system to national economic development, it can be concluded that a sound banking system is fundamental to the workings of any modern economy.

Currently, there are three major groups of banks in Nigeria as per CBN, 2013 reports. They are as follows:

1.   Group A (Tier 1) Banks – Banks of Systemic Importance (8 Banks)
2.   Group B Banks – Banks Acquired by the Assets Management Company of Nigeria (AMCON) (3 Banks)
3.   Group C (Tier 2) Banks – Other Banks (10 Banks).

It is instructive to note that CBN (2013) designated the eight banks in Group A as banks of systemic importance due to the fact that they are regarded as "too big to fail". They include the following banks:

1.   First Bank of Nigeria Limited.
2.   Guaranty Trust Bank Plc.
3.   Zenith Bank Plc.

4. United Bank for Africa Plc.
5. Access Bank Plc.
6. Skye Bank Plc.
7. Ecobank Nigeria.
8. Diamond Bank Plc.

It is further instructive to note that the banks were so designated by the CBN because the failure of any one of them could have a significant multiplier or ripple effect on the entire banking industry and by implication, the entire Nigerian economy. Also, these banks of systemic importance account for approximately 75 per cent of the banking industry in terms of earnings, profitability, asset base, customer deposits and branch network (CBN, 2013).

Group B banks, on the other hand, are those that had significant liquidity and associated problems and were eventually acquired by AMCON with the support of the CBN to ensure that they were not allowed to fail. These banks are:

I. Mainstreet Bank.
II. Keystone Bank.
III. Enterprise Bank.

Group C (Tier 2) banks are the other banking operators in the Nigerian financial system that are classified as non-systemic banks as their failure will affect the financial industry and livelihood of the investing and borrowing public, but to a much limited extent. These banks include the following:

1. Citibank Nigeria Limited.
2. Fidelity Bank Plc.
3. First City Monument Bank Plc.
4. Heritage Banking Company Ltd.
5. Stanbic IBTC Bank Ltd.
6. Standard Chartered Bank Nigeria Ltd.
7. Sterling Bank Plc.
8. Union Bank of Nigeria Plc.
9. Unity Bank Plc.
10. Wema Bank Plc.

It is instructive to note that the non-interest bank in the country (Jaiz Bank) is excluded from the list as it does not engage in conventional banking like the others.

2.4.2 The Philosophy of Banking Reforms in Nigeria

According to Sanusi (2012), economic reforms are undertaken to ensure that every part of the Nigerian economy functions efficiently in order to ensure the achievement of macroeconomic goals of price stability, full employment, high economic growth and internal and external balances. Thus, banking reform in Nigeria is an integral part of the country-wide reform programme undertaken to reposition the Nigerian economy to achieve the objective of becoming one of the 20 largest economies by the year 2020. It is expected therefore that Nigerian banks should be able to compete internationally based on the level of services rendered in the economy as well as the degree to which they comply with best practices especially in the areas of corporate governance and disclosure of information. This is further heightened by the lessons learned from the global financial and economic crises which affected all countries of the world in the periods 2007-2009. Thus all regulators world-wide have seen the need for on-going reforms in the financial sector in order to minimize the impact of any financial down turn that may occur any time in the future (Sanusi, 2012).

2.4.3 Establishment of the Asset Management Corporation of Nigeria (AMCON)

According to Sanusi (2012), the Asset Management Corporation of Nigeria AMCON was established in the year 2010 to specially address the problem of non-performing loans in the Nigerian banking industry, among others. In line with its mandate, it acquired the non-performing risk assets of some of the banks worth over N1.7 trillion. The objective was to achieve a significant boost in the liquidity of the banks as well as enhance their safety and soundness. Consequently, the intervention of AMCON reduced the ratio of non-performing loans (NPL) to total credit significantly from 34.4 per cent in November 2010 to 4.95 per cent as at December 2011.

Sanusi (2012) further stated that in order to ensure that AMCON achieved its mandate, the CBN and all the deposit money banks signed a Memorandum of Understanding (MOU) on the financing of AMCON. The CBN committed itself to contribute N50 billion annually to AMCON, while each of the participating banks was required to contribute an amount equivalent to 0.3 per cent of its total assets annually into a sinking fund as at the date of their audited financial statement for the immediate preceding financial year. The objective of this funding arrangement was to reduce to the barest minimum the impact of the cost of resolving the liquidity crisis on the Nigerian taxpayer.

Also, to further create public confidence in the banking system and enhance customer protection, the CBN established the Consumer and Financial Protection Division to provide a platform for consumers to seek redress. In the first three months of its operation, the Division received over 600 consumer complaints. This was a manifestation of the absence of an effective consumer complaints resolution mechanism in the banks. The CBN has also issued a directive to banks to establish Customer Help Desks at their head offices and branches (Sanusi, 2012).

It is instructive to note that the CBN has further taken steps to integrate the banking system into global best practices in financial reporting and disclosure through the adoption of the International Financial Reporting Standards (IFRS) in the Nigerian banking industry by the end of 2010. It is expected that this would help to promote market discipline and reduce uncertainties which limit the risk of contagion and the concomitant loss that can be suffered by ordinary savers in the economy and investors (Ajakaiye & Olowookere, 2013). Furthermore, the Universal Banking (UB) model adopted in 2001 allowed banks to diversify into non-bank financial businesses and as a result of the consolidation programme, banks were awash with capital. As a consequence, some bank operators abused the laudable objectives of the UB Model with banks operating as private equity and venture capital funds to the detriment of core banking practices (Sanusi, 2012).

In order to address the observed challenges, the CBN reviewed the Universal Banking model with a view to directing banks to focus on their core banking business only. Under the new model, licensed banks are authorized to carry out the following types of business:

a.   Commercial banking (with only regional, national or international authorization);
b.   Merchant (investment) banking;

c. Specialized banking (microfinance, mortgage, non-interest banking (regional or national);

d. Development finance institutions (Sanusi, 2012).

It is important to note that the introduction of non-interest banking in Nigeria is expected to usher in new markets and institutional players. In conjunction with the other banking reforms, this will further deepen the nation's financial markets (Nworji, Olagunju, & Adeyanju, 2011; Sanusi, 2012). Indeed, it is on record that the first fully licensed non-interest bank in the country (Jaiz Bank Plc.) started business on Friday, January 6, 2012 (Sanusi, 2012).

Currently, the Nigerian banking industry has decided to reform its cash operations aspects of banking otherwise known as the "Cash less Policy" with a view to significantly reducing the level of cash in circulation in order to ensure that the attendant costs of processing and transporting cash are reduced thereby achieving lower costs of operations for banks. This will certainly dovetail into a lighter cost burden on bank customers who would benefit in the long run. It will also enable the CBN to avoid the high cost of sorting cash as well as the huge cost of printing currency notes for cash operations. Indeed, the direct cost of cash management to the banking industry is estimated to be about N192 billion by 2012. Research has shown that about 90 per cent of withdrawals by bank customers' were typically below N150,000 whereas, only 10 per cent of bank customers who withdrew over N150,000 were responsible for the astronomical rise in the cost of cash management being incurred by the generality of bank customers (Sanusi, 2012).

Furthermore, there are risks involved in keeping or moving large amounts of cash, namely, the high incidence of robberies, rampant cases of vehicular accidents leading to avoidable deaths of bank staff, encouraging corrupt practices and the public's propensity to abuse and mishandle currency notes (Sanusi, 2012). Sanusi further stated that the CBN, in collaboration with the Bankers' Committee, aims to achieve an environment where a higher and an increasing proportion of transactions are carried out through cheques and electronic payments in line with global trends. The enforcement of the Transaction Date plus 2 days otherwise known as T+2 cheque clearing cycle is being stepped up and efforts are on-going to reduce the cycle to Transaction Date plus 1 day otherwise known as T+1.

Based on the interventionist stance of the CBN in the banking industry on August 14, 2009, some of the weak banks had to merge with stronger banks in order to remain competitive in the market. As a result, five out of the eight weak banks merged with other banks while AMCON acquired the three remaining banks. It is instructive to note that the full recapitalization of the five banks was completed in 2011 (Anyanwu & Ogbonna, 2011; Sanusi, 2012).

It has been argued however, that the key financial indicators in Nigeria like the GDP growth rate, Inflation rate, prime lending and deposit rates have not had the desired impact in any significant manner on the real sectors of the Nigerian economy, therefore, real sectorial growth is yet to be witnessed (Ajakaiye & Olowookere, 2013). Part of the principal reason for this is the fact that the present links between the financial and the real sectors of the economy still remain very weak (Ogujiuba & Obiechina, 2011). The International Monetary Fund – IMF (2013) as cited by Enhancing Financial Innovation & Access – EFInA (2013) is of the view that the Central Bank of Nigeria's banking reforms have been largely successful and now serve as a model for both developed and developing countries. According to the IMF, Nigeria's commercial banking system as a whole can absorb most credit and market risk shocks, withstand liquidity pressures, and absorb moderate potential losses. In the view of the IMF, most Nigerian commercial banks are now well capitalized, liquid and profitable.

2.5 Theoretical Framework

This study is anchored on the following core theories:

2.5.1 Agency Theory

Eisenhardt (1989) stated that agency theory is directed at the ubiquitous agency relationship in which one party (the principal) delegates work to another (the agent) who performs that work. The author further goes on to say that agency theory is concerned with resolving two problems that can occur in agency relationships. The first is the agency problem that arises when the desires or goals of the principal and agent conflict and secondly it is difficult or expensive for the principal to verify what the agent actually does. Therefore, the principal is practically unable to verify with a reasonable degree of certainty that the agent has behaved appropriately. The second is the problem of risk sharing that arises when the principal and agent have different risk appetites. The result therefore is that the principal and the agent may prefer different actions because of the different risk preferences. Whereas accountants started using the agency theory in 1978, economists had employed the use of the concept much earlier in 1971 (Eisenhardt, 1989).

Donaldson and Davis (1991) citing Berle and Means (1932) and Pratt and Zeckhauser (1985) stated that agency theory adopts the position that in the modern corporation where share ownership is widely held, managerial actions depart from those required to maximize shareholders' returns. Also, Jensen and Meckling (1976) argued that there will be an agency loss if the returns to the owners fall below what they would have been if the owners had exercised direct control over the corporation and managed it themselves. The agency theory, therefore, underpins this study in the sense that the managements of banks need to disclose the full facts behind the figures to the owners and stakeholders who need to know how well they have managed the business entities entrusted to them. The shareholders and other stakeholders need full disclosure that will enable them to make informed decisions about their organizations. Furthermore, when full disclosure is made, this will help to reduce the information asymmetry that occurs on account of the fact that shareholders do not have daily and unfettered access to the records of the banks in contradistinction to the management who are responsible for the day to day running of the affairs of the banks.

It is instructive to note that the agency theory requires that there should be a contract between the principal and the agent. This should, therefore, reflect the efficient organization of information and risk-bearing costs (Eisenhardt, 1989). In her view, the agency theory provides a unique and empirically testable perspective on problems of cooperative efforts and is a veritable tool that organizational scholars can use in their study of the broad range of principal-agent issues facing firms.

2.5.2 Corporate Governance Theory

Yusoff and Alhaji (2012) citing Mallin (2004) stated that the theory of corporate governance is regarded as a mechanism where a board of directors is a crucial monitoring device to minimize the problems brought about by the principal-agent relationship. Thus the agency theory is seen as the fundamental theory of corporate governance. This has however been extended to cover other areas such as stewardship and stakeholder theories which further evolve into resource dependency, political, legitimacy and social contract theories. These theories discuss the cause and consequence of variables such as the formation of board structure, audit committee, independent non-executive directors and the duties of upper management and their organizational and social responsibilities rather than merely focus on regulatory structures (Yusoff & Alhaji, 2012). These authors further concluded that a mixture of various theories is best used to describe an effective and efficient good governance practice rather than hypothesizing corporate governance based on a sole theory.

2.5.3 Theory of Disclosure

Disclosure is critical to market driven economies as the dichotomy between funds providers and management is very strong. The disclosure theory therefore, stipulates that there must be adequate release of information about the activities of a company (Gernon & Meek, 2001). Also, the extent of disclosure by a company is significantly determined by the structural complexity thereof (Haniffa & Cook, 2002 cited by Hossain, 2008). Additional research has shown that a voluntary disclosure by firms is also influenced by the choice of auditors as business organizations are more likely to use a highly qualified auditor to achieve a higher level of disclosure (Lee, Stokes, Taylor & Walter, 2003). In summary, therefore, the theory of disclosure stipulates that voluntary disclosure mitigates resource misallocation on the capital market by reducing information asymmetries between insiders and investors and the associated cost of capital. It is important to note however, that the existence and magnitude of this effect depend on the perceived credibility of voluntary disclosure (Gu & Li 2007). Other peripheral theories that indirectly underpin this study in one way or the other include signaling theory, theory of timeliness, stakeholders theory, theory of inspired confidence, monitoring cost theory, and stewardship theory.

2.6 Review of Previous Studies

Muhamad, Shahimi, Yahya and Mahzan (2009) in their study of the disclosure quality of governance issues in annual reports of Malaysian companies discovered that Malaysian companies generally complied with the corporate governance standards requirements. These findings are consistent with those of Naser and Nuseibeh (2003) who found a relatively high compliance with mandatory requirements among Saudi companies. Muhamad, Shahimi, Yahya and Mahzan (2009) also discovered that three factors namely, leverage, size and type of industry were found to have a relationship with the quality of disclosure by quoted companies.

Rahman (2012), on the other hand studied the key factors that influence disclosure credibility of corporate managers. The study found that investors typically examine four basic factors (the situational incentives at the time of the disclosure, management's trustworthiness and competence, the degree of assurance for the message from internal and external sources, and several characteristics of the disclosure such as its precision, venue of release and time horizon) in the process of determining the credibility of management disclosure.

Abiola and Ojo (2012), on the other hand, conducted a study on "Compliance with Regulatory Financial Reporting and Corporate Governance Practices in Selected Primary Mortgage Institutions (PMIs)" in Nigeria. The primary objective of their study was to obtain stakeholders' opinion on compliance with regulatory financial reporting requirements by selected PMIs and to determine the quality of returns rendered by them. The study found a dichotomy in perception between the operators (PMIs) and the public. Whereas, the operators rated compliance to be very high, the customers and members of the public rated compliance to be very low.

Barako, Hancock and Izan, (2006) also conducted a study on the relationship between corporate governance attributes and voluntary disclosures in annual reports in Kenya. They posited that corporate financial reporting is an important part of the process of building investors' confidence. They adopted the agency theory as the framework for their study and also used the Ordinary Least Squares (OLS) with Panel-Corrected Standard Errors (PCSEs) as their methodology. The authors found that the presence of an audit committee is a significant factor associated with the level of voluntary disclosure, and the proportion of non-executive directors on the board is found to be significantly negatively associated with the extent of voluntary disclosure. The study also revealed that board leadership structure did not appear to have a significant influence on the level of voluntary disclosure by companies operating in the Kenyan market.

Awotundun and Kehinde (2011) investigated the theory of corporate governance and stakeholders' interest in ten selected Nigerian banks over a period of ten years (1998-2008). The study adopted the stakeholders approach within the framework of the corporate governance theory to check the soundness of the applicability of the principle of corporate governance in the banking industry with respect to equitable treatment of shareholders and fair treatment of the other stakeholders in the banking industry. Their study showed that corporate governance was not effective in most Nigerian banks. This is based, in part, on the fact that the amount allocated to the providers of funds (shareholders) is insignificant compared to the gross earnings over the years. They were also of the view that shareholders had not been fairly treated by the management of the selected banks.

Uyar and Kilic (2012) conducted a study of Turkish corporations in order to determine the extent of forward-looking information disclosure in publicly traded Turkish corporations, and to identify drivers of disclosure. Through content analysis of annual reports, they concluded that the level of forward-looking disclosure was low among Turkish companies as the companies surveyed were reluctant to disclose bad news even though they were almost always too eager to disclose good news. The results of their study also showed that firms' and auditor sizes were the significant variables in explaining forward-looking information disclosure levels. All other variables like profitability, leverage, ownership structure, independent directors, listing age, are insignificant in the Turkish business environment.

Dabor and Adeyemi (2009) conducted a study to determine the nexus between corporate governance and the credibility of financial statements in Nigeria. They collected primary data from 248 respondents and secondary data from 20 companies that were quoted on the Nigerian Stock Exchange (NSE). Their study revealed that including non-executive directors on the board and complying with requirements of audit committee set-up as mandated by the Companies and Allied

Matters Act, 1990 (as amended), are likely to enhance the credibility of financial statements in the country. The authors however, did not find any evidence to show that Chief Executive Officer (CEO) duality or the absence of institutional investors would hamper the credibility of financial reporting. These findings partially agree with the findings of Dey (2005) who, studying the United States business environment, found that most aspects of governance, in particular, the composition and functioning of the board of directors, the CEO's dual role as the chairman of the board, the effectiveness of the audit committee, and shareholder rights are significantly associated with the credibility of reported earnings for firms with high agency costs.

A summary of the relevant literature reviewed as part of this present study is presented below in table 2.2.

Table 2.2. Summary of Relevant Literature

S/N	Author's Name & Country of Study	Research Objective	Methodology	Result
1	Singhvi & Desai (1971) United States of America (USA)	The study was conducted in order to identify some of the characteristics of corporations in the United States which are associated with, and the probable implications of, the quality of corporate disclosure.	The study examined 100 listed and 55 unlisted corporations for fiscal years ending between April 01, 1965 and March 31, 1966. Annual reports of the listed companies were selected by taking a random sample from the 500 largest United States industrial corporations included in the Fortune's directory of 1965. The unlisted companies were selected, using a systematic sampling procedure from the National Over-the-Counter quotations of about 800 corporations published in the New York Times. A disclosure index of 34 items was used to evaluate the quality of information disclosed in the annual reports. The weighted methodology was also adopted in the study. Results significant at 0.01 level of Chi Square test were reported followed by a detailed multivariate analysis.	The study revealed that companies which disclose inadequate information are likely to be small in size and free from listing requirements. Also, such companies tend to be audited by small accounting firms and are usually less profitable.

| 2 | Stephen Owusu-Ansah, (1998)

Zimbabwe | Examined the impact of corporate attributes on the extent of mandatory disclosure and reporting by listed companies in Zimbabwe | A sample of 49 listed companies were selected for the study using a disclosure index which consisted of 214 mandatory information items. Also, a multivariate regression methodology was adopted in the study. | The study found that companies use financial statements as a signaling tool to express their expectations and intentions. Also, the study found that company size, ownership structure, company age, multinational corporation affiliation, and profitability have a statistically significant positive effect on mandatory disclosure and reporting practices of companies. |

3	Naser & Nuseibeh (2003) Saudi Arabia	The study was undertaken to assess the quality of disclosure by the sampled companies. The study also compared the extent of corporate disclosure before and after the creation of the Saudi Organization of Certified Public Accountants (SOCPA).	Annual reports of 63% and 69% respectively of companies listed on the Saudi Stock Exchange were analysed in 1992 and 1999. Information disclosed was classified into three main categories: mandatory; voluntary related to mandatory; and voluntary unrelated to mandatory disclosure. The study adopted both the weighted and un-weighted approaches and reported the results.	The study found a relatively high compliance by companies with mandatory disclosure requirements.
4	Mendes-Da-Silva & Christensen (2004) Brazil	Examined the determinants of voluntary disclosure of financial information published on the Internet.	The authors carried out a cross sectional study of 291 Brazilian companies.	The study found higher levels of voluntary financial information disclosure by poorly performing companies.

| 5 | Dey, Aiyesha (2005)

United States of America (USA) | Study examined whether the quality of corporate governance of a firm is associated with how credible investors perceive its reported earnings numbers to be. | Reported earnings were measured by the volatility of stock returns in earnings announcement periods (a non-directional measure), and the earnings announcement period excess returns (a directional measure). Adopting several proxies for agency costs, 3 groups of firms were formed and analysed using the principal components analysis procedure on 23 governance variables. | The study found that most aspects of governance, in particular, the composition and functioning of the board of directors, the CEO's dual role as the chairman of the board, the effectiveness of the audit committee, and shareholder rights are significantly associated with the credibility of disclosed earnings for firms with high agency costs. |

| 6 | Karim & Ahmed (2005) Bangladesh | Examined the level of disclosure of financial information upon adoption of International Accounting Standards (IASs) in Bangladesh and the nexus between selected corporate attributes and levels of disclosure in corporate annual reports. | The study adopted the un-weighted methodology using a disclosure index comprising 411 items applied to 188 corporate annual reports 2003. Data was analysed using multiple linear regression models | The study revealed that corporate size, profitability, stock exchange security category, international link of company's auditor and multinational subsidiaries are all significantly associated with the extent of disclosure. |

| 7 | Barako, Hancock & Izan (2006)

Kenya | Examined the relationship between corporate governance attributes and voluntary disclosures in annual reports in the Kenyan economy. | The authors adopted the agency theory as the framework for their study and also used the Ordinary Least Square (OLS) technique with Panel-Corrected Standard Errors (PCSEs) as their methodology. | The authors found that the presence of an audit committee is a significant factor associated with the level of voluntary disclosure, and the proportion of non-executive directors on the board is found to be significantly negatively associated with the extent of voluntary disclosure. The study also revealed that board leadership structure did not appear to have a significant influence on the level of voluntary disclosure by companies operating in the Kenyan market. |
|---|---|---|---|---|

| 8 | Hossain (2008) India | This study examined the extent of both mandatory and voluntary disclosure by listed banking companies in India. It also investigated the nexus between company-specific attributes and total disclosure. | The study considered all 38 banking companies registered on the Indian Stock Exchange. Also, a total of 184 disclosure items were selected out of which 101 and 81 were mandatory and voluntary respectively. A dichotomous approach was adopted in the study. Annual reports for the year 2002-03 were reviewed and the un-weighted disclosure index methodology was adopted in conjunction with the Ordinary Least Squares (OLS) regression technique. | The study revealed that size, profitability, board composition, and market discipline variables are significant, and other variables such as age, complexity of business and asset-in-place are insignificant in explaining the level of disclosure. The results also indicate that Indian banks are very compliant with the rules regarding mandatory disclosure. In contrast, they are far behind in disclosing voluntary items. |

9	Dabor & Adeyemi (2009) Nigeria	The study was conducted to determine the nexus between corporate governance and the credibility of financial statements in Nigeria.	The authors collected primary data from 248 respondents and secondary data from 20 companies that were quoted on the Nigerian Stock Exchange (NSE).	The study revealed that including non-executive directors on the board and complying with requirements of audit committee set-up as mandated by the Companies and Allied Matters Act, 1990 (as amended) are likely to enhance the credibility of financial statements in the country. The study did not find any evidence to show that Chief Executive Officer (CEO) duality or the absence of institutional investors would hamper the credibility of financial reporting.

| 10 | Muhamad, Shahimi, Yahya, & Mahzan (2009)

Malaysia | The study was undertaken to provide evidence on the disclosure quality of governance issues in annual reports of Malaysian companies | Secondary data was used in this study. A disclosure index was established following the Bursa Malaysia Governance Model, the Code's guidelines and Committee of Sponsoring Organizations of the Treadway Commission (COSO) guidelines. A sample of 159 companies for year 2006 was chosen randomly. The data were analysed using: (1) Descriptive statistics and (2) Multivariate test (Multiple Regression Analysis). | The study discovered that Malaysian companies generally complied with the corporate governance standards requirements. Also, the authors discovered that three factors, namely, leverage, size and type of industry were found to have a relationship with the quality of disclosure by quoted companies. |
| 11 | Awotundun & Kehinde (2011)

Nigeria | The study was undertaken to check the soundness of the applicability of the principle of corporate governance in the banking industry | The study investigated the theory of corporate governance and stake-holders' interest in ten selected Nigerian Banks over a period of ten years (1998-2008). It adopted the stakeholders approach within the framework of the corporate governance theory. | Their study revealed that corporate governance was not effective in most Nigerian banks. |

| 12 | Uyar & Kilic (2012)

Turkey | The study was conducted to determine the extent of forward-looking information disclosure in publicly traded Turkish corporations, and to identify drivers of disclosure. | The study was conducted using the methodology of content analysis of annual reports. | The study revealed a low level of forward-looking disclosure amongst Turkish companies as the companies surveyed were reluctant to disclose bad news even though they were almost always too eager to disclose good news. The study also revealed that firms' size and auditor size were the significant variables in explaining forward-looking information disclosure levels. |

| 13 | Abiola & Ojo (2012) Nigeria | The primary objective of the study was to obtain stakeholders' opinion on compliance with regulatory financial reporting requirements by selected Primary Mortgage Institutions (PMIs) and to determine the quality of returns rendered by them. | The methodology of judgmental sampling through delivery and collection of questionnaires targeted at three stakeholders groups was used. In all, 6 PMIs were selected based on convenience and location, accounting for more than 30% of the Total Assets of N329.8 billion. A simple regression technique was used for the analysis. | The study found a dichotomy in perception between the operators (PMIs) and the public. Whereas, the operators rated compliance to be very high, the customers and members of the public rated compliance to be very low. |

| 14 | Enofe & Isiavwe (2012)

Nigeria | This study evaluated the extent to which banks in Nigeria comply with best practices in the performance of the financial accounting and disclosure function with a special focus on corporate governance and corporate disclosure. | Secondary data were collected from fourteen banks and analyzed using the Ordinary Least Squares (OLS) regression technique due to its high degree of unbiasedness, efficiency and consistency. | The results showed that banks in Nigeria have generally maintained a high standard of information disclosure for the year 2010. Also, the study showed a strong positive relationship between bank profitability and disclosure of information. The study further showed that the size of the board with financial expertise has a significant influence on the disclosure of information in the annual report. |

| 15 | Sheehan Rahman (2012)

United Kingdom (UK) | The research was undertaken to ascertain the key factors that influence disclosure credibility of corporate managers. | Exploratory research methodology was adopted involving a review and critique of extant literature. | The study found that investors typically examine four basic factors (the situational incentives at the time of the disclosure, management's trustworthiness and competence, the degree of assurance for the message from internal and external sources, and several characteristics of the disclosure such as its precision, venue of release and time horizon) in the process of determining the credibility of management disclosure. |

| 16 | Lan, Wang and Zhang (2013) China | Examined the determinants and features of voluntary disclosure based on information in the annual reports of Chinese firms listed on the Shanghai and Shenzhen Stock Exchanges. | A disclosure index of 119 items was developed using a two-step approach. This was followed by applying a dichotomous methodology of assigning 1 or 0 to the various items using the unweighted methodology. In all, 1,066 firms were selected from both Stock Exchanges at the end of 2006 representing 80% of the quoted companies. Banks and insurance firms were excluded because their financial reports were not comparable with those of firms in other industries. Data was analysed using the OLS model as a multivariate test to assess the effect on each of the variables. | Study revealed that voluntary disclosure in China is positively related to firm size, leverage, assets-in-place and return on equity and is negatively related to auditor type and the level of maturity or sophistication of the intermediary and legal environments. The study also showed some evidence to suggest a quadratic convex association between state ownership and voluntary disclosure. |

Source: Compiled by the researcher (2014)

CHAPTER THREE

MATERIALS AND METHODS

3.1 Introduction

This chapter looks at the methodology adopted in the conduct of this study. Specific areas of coverage include the research design, population and sample frame, sources of data, model specification and data analysis procedures. In all, the chapter succinctly presents the approach that was adopted in a bid to achieve, in an empirical manner, the desired objectives of the study.

3.2 Research Design

The research design adopted in this work is the longitudinal (panel) research design in order to fully investigate and analyze the time series data for the period (2005 – 2013) involved in the study. This design was considered appropriate as it enabled the researcher to obtain in-depth knowledge of the determinants of corporate disclosure by banks in Nigeria. All the twenty one deposit money banks operating in the country as at December 31, 2013 were considered for the purpose of the study.

3.3 Population and Sample Frame

The population consists of all twenty one (21) banks licensed by the Central Bank of Nigeria to operate as Deposit Money Banks (DMBs) as at 2013. For the purpose of the study however, only nineteen banks were used as two of the banks (Heritage Bank and Enterprise Bank) did not have the relevant data required for the study. A list of the nineteen banks used for the study is presented as Appendix 1.

3.4 Sources of Data

Data for disclosure index was obtained from key sources like the CBN Code of Corporate Governance as well as the Corporate Governance Code by SEC and other reports like the Nigerian Banks Financial Transparency reports. In addition, the annual reports for all the banks for the period 2005 - 2013 were reviewed to obtain key data required for the study.

3.5 Review of Related Models

As part of efforts to develop an appropriate model for this study, a careful examination of relevant empirical models used in past studies is presented below.

3.5.1 Hossain (2008) Model

This study focused on the banking industry in India. On 30th June 2004, the total number of banking companies listed on the Bombay Stock Exchange (BSE) and the National Stock Exchange (NSE) was 38, out of which 18 were public sector and 20 private sector banks. Although, there are 23 recognized stock exchanges in India, the study considered only the BSE and NSE; the reason being that the BSE is India's second largest stock exchange while the NSE was established as a model exchange to provide nation-wide services to investors. Thus, the Actual sample represents about 100% of the population of banking companies listed on the stock exchanges.

Annual reports for the year 2002-03 were collected and analysed and the following Ordinary Least Squares (OLS) regression model was fitted to the data in order to assess the effect of each variable on the disclosure level:

$$Y = \beta 0 + \beta 1X1 + \beta 2X2 + \beta 3X3 + \beta 4X4 + \beta 5X5 + \beta 6X6 + \beta 7X7 + \beta 8X8 + e$$

Where Y = total disclosure score received for each bank
$\beta 0$ = the intercept; e = the error term

3.5.2. Singhvi & Desai (1971) Model

This model, tagged adequate corporate disclosure model was developed with the objective of identifying some of the characteristics of corporations in the United States which are associated with the quality of corporate disclosure. 100 listed and 55 unlisted corporations for fiscal years ending between April 01, 1965 and March 31, 1966 were analysed. Annual reports of the listed companies were selected by taking a random sample from the 500 largest United States industrial corporations included in the Fortune's Directory of 1965. A disclosure index of 34 items was used to evaluate the quality of information disclosed in the annual reports using the "weighted" methodology.

The model which includes information on financial and non-financial matters related to the past, present and future of the corporation was specified as follows:

$$I = f (A,N,L,C,R,E)\dots\dots\dots\dots\dots\dots\dots\dots\dots\dots\dots\dots\dots\dots\dots\dots\dots\dots\dots 1$$

Where,

I = Index of quality of disclosure.
A = Assets in billions of dollars
N = Number of stockholders in thousands
L = Listing status: (L=1=listed; L=0=Unlisted)
C = CPA Firm (C=1= Large Firm; C=0= Small Firm)
R = Rate of return in percentage
E = Earnings margin in percentage

The authors further developed the following model to quantify the conceptualized relationship between the price dispersion and the quality of disclosure:

$$P = C_1 - C_2 (I) \dots\dots\dots 2$$

Where,

P= Percentage Price Dispersion
C_1 = Constant > 0
C_2 = Constant > 0
I = Index of quality of disclosure

3.5.3 Karim and Ahmed (2005) Model

This model was designed to examine the level of disclosure of financial information upon adoption of International Accounting Standards (IASs) in Bangladesh and the nexus between selected corporate attributes and levels of disclosure in corporate annual reports. The study adopted the un-weighted methodology using a disclosure index comprising 411 items and applied to 188 corporate annual reports in 2003. Both financial and non-financial data were analysed using multiple linear regression models which are specified as follows:

ODI = a + b1 LOGASSET + b2 ROE + b3 AUDITOR + b4 MNCSUBSI + b5 ACCOUNTT +

b6 FIN + b7 MKTCAT + e$\dots\dots\dots$1

The model which was based on the nonfinancial services sector companies was:

ODI = a + b1 LOGASSET + b2 ROE + b3 AUDITOR + b4 MNCSUBSI + b5

ACCOUNTT + b6 EVERAGE + b7 MKTCAT + e$\dots\dots$2

Where:

ODI   = Overall Disclosure Index

AUDITOR	=	Large audit firms with an international link
LOGASSET	=	Natural log of total assets (in million Tk))
ROE	=	Return on assets (in million Tk)
MNCSUBSI	=	Subsidiary of a multinational company
ACCOUNTT	=	Qualified accountant employed
FIN	=	Financial sector company
LEVERAGE	=	Debt to equity ratio
MKTCAT	=	Market category

It is instructive to note that these models (above) formed a critical ingredient in the determination of the model adopted for this study.

3.6 Model Specification

In the study of disclosure levels, the methodology adopted typically revolves around the two main approaches of weighted and un-weighted disclosure indices (Hossain, 2008). With the weighted approach, specific weights are assigned to items that are disclosed. These range from zero (assigned to items that are not disclosed) to "1" depending on the significance of the item. The un-weighted approach however, adopts a uniform level of significance for all of the disclosure items. Thus, a dichotomous approach is adopted where items disclosed are assigned a value of "1" whereas items not disclosed are assigned a value of "0".

For the purpose of this study, the un-weighted approach was adopted. This is based on the fact that all items of disclosure are considered equally important.

Furthermore, previous research in this area has shown that there is very little or no difference in the final outcome whether or not weights are assigned to items of disclosure in the annual report (Hossain, 2008). The un-weighted disclosure method or approach therefore, measures the total disclosure score in an additive manner. This study adopted the

Hossain (2008) model reviewed above. Thus, the Ordinary Least Squares (OLS) regression technique was used due to its fundamental properties of unbiasedness, efficiency and consistency. The following model was therefore used in this study to capture the influence of the respective attributes on corporate disclosure in the Nigerian banks:

$$DISINDEX = \beta0 + \beta1TASSETS + \beta2AGE + \beta3PAT + B4FINEXP + \beta5INTSUB + \beta_6BOARDIND + \varepsilon_j$$

Where;

DISINDEX = Disclosure Index
TASSETS = Firm Size
AGE = Bank Age
PAT = Profitability
FINEXP = Financial Expertise
INTSUB = International Subsidiaries
BOARDIND = Board Independence
ε_j = Error term

3.6.1 Measurement of Variables

In the model specified by Cooke (1992) and utilized by Hossain (2008), total disclosure is measured as follows:

$$TD = \sum_{i=1}^{n} di$$

Where:

d = 1, if the item d_i is disclosed
0 = if the item is not disclosed.
n = number of items

The table below shows the definition of the different variables used in the study as well as their codes, proxies, and signs. This undoubtedly helps to provide further clarity into the variables used in the model adopted for this study.

Table 3.1. DEFINITION OF VARIABLES AND EXPECTED SIGNS

VARIABLES	CODE	PROXY	SIGN
Disclosure Index	DISINDEX	Corporate Disclosure Index based on combined risk management and corporate governance disclosures by Banks.	
Bank (Firm) Size	TASSETS	Logarithm of Total Assets	+
Bank Age	AGE	Total number of years a bank has been in existence	+
Profitability	PAT	Profit After Tax	+
Financial Expertise	FINEXP	Number of directors on the board with financial expertise	+
International Subsidiaries	INTSUB	A dichotomous variable equal to 1 if there is an international subsidiary owned by the bank otherwise 0.	+
Board Independence	BOARDIND	Ratio of Non-executive directors to board size	+

Source: Compiled by the researcher (2014)

3.6 Data Analysis

Relevant data analysed for this study were obtained from various sources including the annual reports of banks for the period in question, Companies and Allied Matters Act (1991) as amended, the SEC and CBN Corporate Governance Codes. A dichotomous methodology was used in which the disclosure items were assigned a score of "1" if they were reported or a value of "0" if they were not reported. This methodology is called the unweighted approach (Hossain, 2008). With this methodology, all items of disclosure are deemed to be of equal importance to the consumer of the financial reports.

In order to ensure reliability and validity of the empirical result, some diagnostic tests were also conducted. The diagnostic tests include multicollinearity, heteroskedasticity and autocorrelation.

Multicolinearity

This is a situation that may occur in multiple regression analysis where some or all of the explanatory variables are highly intercorrelated. When multicolinearity occurs, then a basic assumption for the use of general regression analysis technique as is the case with the current study may be violated. In order to test for the presence of multicolinearity in the model, the variance inflation factor (VIF) was used.

Heteroskedasticity

Normally, the Ordinary Least Squares (OLS) makes the assumption that the variance of the error is constant or homoscedastic. If the error terms do not have a constant variance, they are termed heteroskedastic. The consequences of ignoring heteroskedasticity in a study of this nature would imply that the OLS estimates are no longer Best Linear Unbiased Estimates (BLUE). An example of the heteroskedasticity test is the Breusch-Pagan-Godfrey test.

Serial correlation Test

Serial correlation occurs when the error terms from different time periods are correlated. More often it occurs in time series studies. If there is a presence of autocorrelation in the model, then the coefficient estimate will no longer be Best, Linear, Unbiased Estimate (BLUE). This may generate wrong inferences about a variable as to its significance in a study. One common test for the presence of serial correlation is the Durbin-Watson test which was also used as a part of the analysis of the data gathered in this study.

CHAPTER FOUR

FINDINGS/RESULTS

4.1 Introduction

This chapter deals with the presentation and analysis of the results obtained from the statistical analysis of data gathered in this study. The primary objective of this study was to evaluate the determinants of corporate disclosure by bank operators in Nigeria with a special focus on financial statement disclosure. Data used were obtained from the annual reports of the various banks for the period 2005 - 2013. During the course of the study, a checklist (the disclosure index) was constructed for the purpose of evaluating the content of the annual reports. The un-weighted scoring approach was adopted for the scoring. This approach is preferred since it is based on the assumption that each item disclosed in the financial statements is of equal importance with every other item that is disclosed. This, therefore, reduces subjectivity and provides a neutral assessment of the various items of disclosure.

Panel design was also adopted for the study. This is because the study combines time series and cross-sectional data for the sampled banks over a period of nine years from 2005 - 2013. The variables used in the model include Disclosure Index (DISINDEX) as the dependent variable while the independent variables include Banks' age (AGE), Board Independence (BOARDIND), Profitability (PAT), International Subsidiaries (INTSUB), Financial Expertise (FINEXP) and Bank

Size (TASSETS). The study used Descriptive Statistics, Correlation Analysis, pooled and panel regression analysis as well as other diagnostic tests. The model was estimated with the aid of a computer software (E-views 8.0).

4.2 Descriptive Statistics

The result from the descriptive statistics is presented in the table below:

Table 4.1. Descriptive Statistics

	DISINDEX	TASSETS	AGE	PAT	FINEXP	INTSUB	BOARDIND
Mean	173.4444	1.59E+09	31.39181	3.83E+09	5.90643	0.578947	0.7228
Median	137	6.02E+08	22	17077918	6	1	0.625
Maximum	196	3.12E+10	119	9.58E+10	7	1	0.75
Minimum	188	25229804	13	-1.4E+07	3	0	0.542857
Std. Dev.	27.41492	3.61E+09	25.28738	1.56E+10	17.35723	0.495178	1.095494
Skewness	-0.075195	5.893731	2.423251	4.742996	2.144336	0.319801	4.908905
Kurtosis	2.162582	43.29036	7.885712	24.89855	6.566654	1.102273	25.61383
Jarque-Bera	5.157694	12556.08	337.4312	4057.904	221.6853	28.57453	4330.395
Probability	0.075861	0	0	0	0	0.000001	0

Source: Researcher's computation (2014)

Table 4.1. shows the descriptive statistics of the variables used in the analysis. The table shows that the maximum disclosure score was 196 while the minimum disclosure score was 188. The average disclosure score of the banks was about 173 out of the 219 items in the disclosure index developed for this study. The result shows that the average age of the banks was about 31 years while the average number of directors with financial expertise on the board was about 6. The results further show that on the average, about 58% of banks with headquarters in Nigeria have international subsidiaries. Also, the maximum level of independence of the board as exemplified by the presence of non-executive directors was about 75% whereas the minimum level of independence was about 54% with an average board independence level of about 62%.

The descriptive statistics revealed that most of the variables used in the study were normally distributed as observed from the Jarque-Bera statistics.

4.3 Correlation Analysis

The result from the correlation analysis is shown in the table below:

Table 4.2. Pearson's Product Moment Correlation Matrix

Correlation t-Statistic Probability	DISINDEX	TASSETS	AGE	PAT	FINEXP	INTSUB	BOARDIND
DISINDEX	1.000000						

TASSETS	0.165490	1.000000					
	2.181445	-----					
	0.0305	-----					
AGE	0.045001	0.245637	1.000000				
	0.585612	3.294205	-----				
	0.5589	0.0012	-----				
PAT	0.226912	0.039994	0.091734	1.000000			
	3.028859	0.520333	1.197591	-----			
	0.0028	0.6035	0.2328	-----			
FINEXP	0.242961	0.164248	0.340232	0.095731	1.000000		
	3.256061	2.164627	4.703631	1.250249	-----		
	0.0014	0.0318	0.0000	0.2129	-----		
INTSUB	0.373950	0.130738	0.200187	0.207215	0.227040	1.000000	
	5.241637	1.714310	2.656196	2.753564	3.030669	-----	
	0.0000	0.0883	0.0087	0.0065	0.0028	-----	
BOARDIND	0.145980	0.013275	0.003556	0.053646	0.224475	0.237789	1.000000
	1.918286	0.172592	0.046229	0.698402	2.994600	3.182546	-----
	0.0568	0.8632	0.9632	0.4859	0.0032	0.0017	-----

Source: Researcher's computation (2014)

Table 4.2. shows that the co-efficient of correlation of a variable with respect to itself is 1.000. This indicates that there exists a perfect correlation between a variable with respect to itself. The relationships amongst the variables are discussed below:

There exists a positive relationship between the level of disclosure and size of the banks (TASSETS) with a correlation co-efficient of 0.16 which means that the strength of relationship between them is about 16%. The results also show that there exists a positive relationship between the level of disclosure and age of the banks (AGE) with a correlation co-efficient of 0.04 which means that the strength of relationship between them is about 4%. PAT with a co-efficient of 0.22 means that there exists a direct relationship between performance of the bank and the level of disclosure. FINEXP with a co-efficient of 0.24 shows that there exists a positive relationship between the number of directors with financial expertise and the level of disclosure. INTSUB and BOARDIND with a co-efficient of 0.37 and 0.14 also show a direct relationship between international subsidiaries and board independence with level of disclosure. From the correlation analysis, it was observed that all the variables had a direct relationship with the level of disclosure.

4.4 Analysis of Variance (ANOVA)

The study carried out analysis of variance in order to find out if there exists a significant difference in the disclosure levels of Nigerian banks. The result from the analysis of variance is shown in the table below:

Table 4.3. Test for Equality of Disclosure Index

Method	df	Value	Probability
Anova F-test	(6, 1242)	10.12697	0.0000
Welch F-test*	(6, 496.21)	898.1744	0.0000

Source: Researcher's computation (2014)

The result from the analysis of variance depicted in table 4.3. shows the ANOVA F-test and Welch F-test with calculated F-values of 10.12 and 898.17 with p-values of 0.000 respectively which indicate that there exists a significant difference in the disclosure practices of Nigerian banks.

4.5 Granger Causality

In order to find out if there exists a bi-directional relationship among the variables, the study used the Granger causality. The result for the Granger causality is shown below:

Table 4.4. Granger Causality Test

Null Hypothesis:	F-Statistic	Prob.
TASSETS does not Granger Cause DISINDEX	1.11526	0.3308
DISINDEX does not Granger Cause TASSETS	0.38522	0.681
AGE does not Granger Cause DISINDEX	1.32750	0.2686
DISINDEX does not Granger Cause AGE	0.45383	0.6362
PAT does not Granger Cause DISINDEX	0.71476	0.4912
DISINDEX does not Granger Cause PAT	1.71092	0.1847
FINEXP does not Granger Cause DISINDEX	0.87992	0.4173
DISINDEX does not Granger Cause FINEXP	0.38209	0.6832
INTSUB does not Granger Cause DISINDEX	2.23907	0.1105
DISINDEX does not Granger Cause INTSUB	0.00495	0.9951
BOARDIND does not Granger Cause DISINDEX	2.10537	0.126
DISINDEX does not Granger Cause BOARDIND	1.45968	0.2362

Source: Researcher's computation (2014)

The result of the granger causality shows that the F-statistic with the p-values indicate that none of the variables had a bi-directional relationship with the level of disclosure which implies that the causality that exists among the variables is uni-directional. Thus, we can use a univariate analysis which is presented in the next sub-section.

4.6 Regression Analysis

The result from the pooled regression analysis is shown in table 4.5. below

Table 4.5.   Pooled Regression Analysis

Variable	Coefficient	Std. Error	t-Statistic	Prob.
C	152.3518	4.467028	34.10584	0.0000
TASSETS	1.48E-09	5.46E-10	2.717113	0.0073
AGE	0.025662	0.135585	0.189267	0.8501
PAT	2.65E-10	1.25E-10	2.127193	0.0349
FINEXP	0.311444	0.124800	2.495308	0.0327
INTSUB	18.73239	4.294701	4.361745	0.0000
BOARDIND	0.904986	1.801648	0.502310	0.6161
R-squared	0.424917	Mean dependent var		146.4444
Adjusted R-squared	0.396560	S.D. dependent var		27.41492
S.E. of regression	24.57331	Akaike info criterion		9.281273
Sum squared resid	99030.99	Schwarz criterion		9.409879
Log likelihood	786.5488	Hannan-Quinn criter.		9.333456
F-statistic	7.931702	Durbin-Watson stat		1.662536
Prob(F-statistic)	0.000000			

Source: Researcher's computation (2014)

In table 4.5. above, data for the coefficient of determination (R-square) shows that about 42% of the variation in the level of banks disclosures could be explained by the predictors namely: Board Independence (BOARDIND), age of the bank (AGE), Profitability (PAT), International Subsidiaries (INTSUB), Financial Expertise (FINEXP) and Firm Size (TASSETS) which means that about 58% of the systematic variation in the level of disclosure was left unexplained by the model, hence it was captured by the error term. This implies that other factors apart from bank age, board Independence, profitability, international subsidiaries, financial expertise, and firm size account for the level of disclosure in the Nigerian banking industry.

Furthermore, the F-statistics shows that the overall model was statistically significant, since the calculated F-value of 7.9 (with a p-value of 0.000) is greater than the critical F-value of 2.0 at 5% level of significance. This means that firms' size, bank age, board independence, profitability, presence of international subsidiaries and financial expertise collectively have a significant impact on the level of disclosure in Nigerian banks.

On the basis of the individual statistical significance, as shown by the t-ratios in the table above, it was observed that TASSETS, PAT, FINEXP and INTSUB with t-values of 2.71, 2.12, 2.49 and 4.36 respectively (with p-values of 0.0073, 0.0349, 0.0327 & 0.000 respectively) were greater than the critical t-value of 2.0 at 5% level of significance under the two tailed test. This means that size of the bank, performance of the bank, board members with financial expertise and presence of international subsidiaries are the major determinants of the level of disclosure in Nigerian banks. It was observed that all the variables have a positive relationship with the level of disclosure in Nigerian banks. The Durbin Watson statistics of 1.66 indicates the absence of first order autocorrelation of the stochastic variables inside the error term in the model.

4.7. Panel Regression Analysis

The data were also analysed using the panel least squares estimation technique. Both the Fixed Effect Model and Random Effect Model were analysed. Before presenting the result from the panel data analysis, the Hausman's test was carried out in order to determine whether the Fixed or Random Effect Model is more appropriate. The result from the Hausman's test is presented below:

Table 4.6. Hausman's Test

Test Summary	Chi-Sq. Statistic	Chi-Sq. d.f.	Prob.
Period random	1.611968	6	0.9517

Source: Researcher's computation (2014)

In addition, the Random Effect Model (REM) test was carried out to determine if it was more appropriate than the Fixed Effect Model (FEM) test. From the Chi-square value of 1.61 with a probability value of 0.95, this is greater than the p-value of 0.05. This means that the Random Effect Model is more appropriate than the Fixed Effect Model and thus we would rely more on the Random Effect Model.

4.8. Fixed Effect Model (FEM)

The result from the Fixed Effect Model is presented in the table below:

Table 4.7. Fixed Effect Model

Variable	Coefficient	Std. Error	t-Statistic	Prob.
C	117.1817	15.35340	7.632296	0.0000
TASSETS	1.02E-09	5.40E-10	2.186278	0.0313
AGE	1.230592	0.549939	2.237689	0.0268
PAT	2.51E-11	9.32E-11	0.268938	0.7884
FINEXP	0.224094	0.476851	0.469947	0.6391
INTSUB	2.977129	11.76467	0.253057	0.8006
BOARDIND	0.308095	1.115742	0.276134	0.7828

Effects Specification				
Cross-section fixed (dummy variables)				

R-squared	0.759376	Mean dependent var		146.4444
Adjusted R-squared	0.717889	S.D. dependent var		27.41492
S.E. of regression	14.56119	Akaike info criterion		8.333760
Sum squared resid	30744.08	Schwarz criterion		8.811440
Log likelihood	686.5365	Hannan-Quinn criter.		8.527582
F-statistic	18.30401	Durbin-Watson stat		2.027834
Prob(F-statistic)	0.000000			

Source: Researcher's computation (2014)

Table 4.7. shows the result of the Fixed Effect Model (FEM). It was observed that the coefficient of determination (R-square) with an R-square of 0.75 indicates that about 75% of the Variation in the level of banks' disclosures could be explained by the predictors namely: board independence (BOARDIND), age of the bank (AGE), profitability (PAT), international subsidiaries (INTSUB), financial expertise (FINEXP) and firms' size (TASSETS) which means that about 25% of the systematic variation in the level of disclosure was left unexplained by the model, hence it was captured by the error term. This implies that other factors, apart from bank (firm) size, bank age, board independence, profitability, international subsidiaries and financial expertise, account for the level of disclosure in the Nigerian banking industry.

On the basis of the overall significance of the model as shown by the F-statistics it was observed that the model was statistically significant since the calculated F-statistics of 18.3 is greater than the critical F-value of 2.0 at 5% level of significance. This implies that all the variables have a significant impact on the level of disclosure in Nigerian banks.

On the basis of the individual statistical significance as shown by the t-ratios in the table above, it was observed that TASSETS and AGE with a t-value of 2.1 and 2.2 respectively were greater than the critical t-value of 2.0 at 5% level of significance under the two tailed test. This means that size of the bank and the age thereof are the major determinants of the level of disclosure in Nigerian banks. It was observed that all the variables have a positive relationship with the level of disclosure in Nigerian banks. The Durbin Watson statistics of 2.02 indicates the absence of first order autocorrelation of the stochastic variables inside the error term in the model.

4.9 Random Effect Model (REM)

Table 4.8. Result from Random Effect Model (REM)

Variable	Coefficient	Std. Error	t-Statistic	Prob.
C	153.2300	4.665494	32.84324	0.0000
TASSETS	1.41E-09	5.64E-10	2.495009	0.0136
AGE	0.010975	0.143472	0.076494	0.9391
PAT	2.81E-10	1.30E-10	2.163780	0.0320
FINEXP	0.271333	0.127598	2.122699	0.0343
INTSUB	18.33403	4.418075	4.149778	0.0001
BOARDIND	0.901995	1.875199	0.481013	0.6312

Effects Specification

Period fixed (dummy variables)

R-squared	0.433670	Mean dependent var	146.4444
Adjusted R-squared	0.364897	S.D. dependent var	27.41492
S.E. of regression	25.05284	Akaike info criterion	9.363482
Sum squared resid	97912.57	Schwarz criterion	9.639067
Log likelihood	-785.5777	Hannan-Quinn criter.	9.475303
F-statistic	3.397697	Durbin-Watson stat	1.651911
Prob(F-statistic)	0.000084		

Source: Researcher's computation (2014)

From table 4.8. above, the result from Hausman's test indicates that we should rely more on the result of the Random Effect Model (REM) than of the Fixed Effect Model (FEM). It was observed that the coefficient of determination (R-square) with an R-square value of 0.43 indicates that about 43% of the variation in the level of banks' disclosures could be explained by the predictors namely: board independence (BOARDIND), age of the bank (AGE), profitability (PAT), international subsidiaries (INTSUB), financial expertise (FINEXP) and firms' size (TASSETS) which means that about 57% of the systematic variation in the level of disclosure was left unexplained by the model, hence captured by the error term. This implies that other factors apart from firm size, banks' age, board independence, profitability, international subsidiaries and financial expertise account for the level of disclosure in the Nigerian banking industry.

On the basis of the overall significance of the model as shown by the F-statistics, it was observed that the model was statistically significant since the calculated F-statistics of 3.39 is greater than the critical F-value of 2.0 at 5% level of significance. This implies that all the variables have a significant impact on the level of disclosure in Nigerian banks.

On the basis of the individual statistical significance as shown by the t-ratios in the table above, it was observed that TASSETS, PAT, FINEXP and INTSUB with a t-value of 2.49, 2.16, 2.12 and 4.14 respectively were greater than the critical t-value of 2.0 at 5% level of significance under the two tailed test. This means that size of the bank, performance of the bank, board members with financial expertise and banks with international subsidiaries are the major determinants of the level of disclosure in Nigerian banks. It was also observed that all the variables have a positive relationship with the level of disclosure in Nigerian banks. The Durbin Watson statistics of 1.651 indicates the absence of first order autocorrelation of the stochastic variables inside the error term in the model.

4.10 Diagnostic Tests

In order to ensure the reliability and validity of the result, some diagnostic tests were conducted for multicollinearity, Heteroskedasticity and autocorrelation. In order to test for the presence of multicollinearity in the model, the variance inflation factor (VIF) was carried out. The Heteroskedasticity test was conducted using Breusch-Pagan-Godfrey test while the Breush-Godfrey LM test was conducted to test the presence of autocorrelation in the model. The results are shown below:

4.10.1 Multicollinearity (VIF)

The result from the Variance Inflation Factor (VIF) is shown below:

Table 4.9. Variance Inflation Factor (VIF)

Variable	Coefficient Variance	Uncentered VIF	Centered VIF
C	19.95434	5.650752	NA
TASSETS	2.98E-19	1.305252	1.091086
AGE	0.018383	4.914849	1.303293
PAT	1.55E-20	1.132321	1.067741
FINEXP	0.015575	2.055729	1.321028
INTSUB	18.44446	3.023945	1.273240
BOARDIND	3.245936	1.718981	1.096685

Source: Researcher's computation (2014)

The results from the multicollinearity test conducted with the use of the Variance Inflation Factor shows that there is no problem of multicollinearity among the explanatory variables since the centered VIF values are below the bench mark of 10, indicating the absence of the multicollinearity in the model. This was also confirmed by the correlation matrix which shows a low correlation among the explanatory variables.

4.10.2 Autocorrelation Test

The result from the autocorrelation test is shown below:

Table 4.10. Breusch-Godfrey Serial Correlation LM Test

F-statistic	119.8229	Prob. F(2,162)	0.3544
Obs*R-squared	102.0288	Prob. Chi-Square(2)	0.3423

Source: Researcher's computation (2014)

Table 4.10. shows that the F-statistic and Obs*R-square indicate the absence of autocorrelation in the model since the F-statistic and Obs*R-square with p-values of 0.35 and 0.34 are greater than the critical values at 5% level of significance. Thus, we can conclude that there is no presence of autocorrelation in the model.

4.10.3 Heteroskedasticity Test

The result from the Heteroskedasticity test is shown in the table below:

Table 4.11. Heteroskedasticity Test: Breusch-Pagan-Godfrey

F-statistic	5.186574	Prob. F(6,164)	0.4561
Obs*R-squared	27.27266	Prob. Chi-Square(6)	0.4324
Scaled explained SS	16.40054	Prob. Chi-Square(6)	0.4118

Source: Researcher's computation (2014)

Table 4.11. shows that the F-statistic and Obs*R-square indicate the absence of heteroskedasticity in the model since the F-statistic and Obs*R-square with p-values of 0.45 and 0.43 are greater than the critical values at 5% level of significance. Thus, we can conclude that there is no presence of heteroskedasticity in the model.

4.11 Test of Hypotheses

The hypotheses were tested using the panel regression results. The study adopted 5% level of significance.

Hypothesis 1

Ho1. There is no significant positive relationship between the total assets of banks in Nigeria and the level of disclosure of the banks.

Table 4.12. Test of Hypothesis 1

Variable	Coefficient	Std. Error	t-Statistic	Prob.
C	145.4137	2.239121	64.94231	0.0000
TASSETS	1.19E-09	5.84E-10	2.038271	0.0430

R-squared	0.022808	Mean dependent var	147.2500
Adjusted R-squared	0.017318	S.D. dependent var	27.74341
S.E. of regression	27.50213	Akaike info criterion	9.477453
Sum squared resid	134633.4	Schwarz criterion	9.512930
Log likelihood	-850.9708	Hannan-Quinn criter.	9.491838
F-statistic	4.154550	Durbin-Watson stat	2.362336
Prob(F-statistic)	0.043002		

Source: Researcher's computation (2014)

From the regression result, it was observed that TASSETS with a calculated t-value of 2.03 is greater than the critical t-value of 2.0 at 5% level of significance. Therefore, we reject the null hypothesis and accept the alternative hypothesis which states that there is a significant positive relationship between the total assets of banks in Nigeria and the level of disclosure of the banks.

Hypothesis 2

Ho2. The age of banks operating in Nigeria has no significant impact on the level of disclosure in their annual reports.

Table 4.13. Test of Hypothesis 2

Variable	Coefficient	Std. Error	t-Statistic	Prob.
C	148.2501	3.291108	45.04566	0.0000
AGE	-0.030104	0.076947	-0.391225	0.6961

R-squared	0.000859	Mean dependent var		147.2500
Adjusted R-squared	-0.004754	S.D. dependent var		27.74341
S.E. of regression	27.80928	Akaike info criterion		9.499666
Sum squared resid	137657.4	Schwarz criterion		9.535143
Log likelihood	-852.9699	Hannan-Quinn criter.		9.514050
F-statistic	0.153057	Durbin-Watson stat		2.380726
Prob (F-statistic)	0.696099			

Source: Researcher's computation (2014)

From the regression result, it was observed that AGE with a calculated t-value of -0.39 and a p-value of 0.69 is less than the critical t-value of 2.0 at 5% level of significance. Therefore, we accept the null hypothesis which states that the age of banks operating in Nigeria has no significant impact on the level of disclosure in their annual reports.

Hypothesis 3

Ho3. The performance of Nigerian banks has no significant impact on the level of disclosure in their annual reports.

Table 4.14. Test of Hypothesis 3

Variable	Coefficient	Std. Error	t-Statistic	Prob.
C	148.1793	2.064968	71.75865	0.0000
PAT	4.01E-10	1.31E-10	3.055394	0.0026
R-squared	0.050370	Mean dependent var		146.7022
Adjusted R-squared	0.044975	S.D. dependent var		27.40791
S.E. of regression	26.78448	Akaike info criterion		9.424695
Sum squared resid	126263.9	Schwarz criterion		9.460445
Log likelihood	-836.7978	Hannan-Quinn criter.		9.439193
F-statistic	9.335432	Durbin-Watson stat		1.578210
Prob(F-statistic)	0.002598			

Source: Researcher's computation (2014)

From the regression result, it was observed that PAT with a calculated t-value of 3.05 and a p-value of 0.002 is greater than the critical t-value of 2.0 at 5% level of significance. Therefore, we reject the null hypothesis and accept the alternative hypothesis which states that the performance of Nigerian banks has a significant impact on the level of disclosure in their annual reports.

Hypothesis 4

Ho4. Board members with financial expertise in Nigerian banks have no significant influence on disclosure of information in the annual reports.

Table 4.15. Test of Hypothesis 4

Variable	Coefficient	Std. Error	t-Statistic	Prob.
C	141.7816	2.523606	56.18216	0.0000
FINEXP	0.378036	0.117858	3.207550	0.0016

R-squared	0.056440	Mean dependent var	146.6092
Adjusted R-squared	0.050954	S.D. dependent var	27.42846
S.E. of regression	26.72052	Akaike info criterion	9.420169
Sum squared resid	122805.7	Schwarz criterion	9.456480
Log likelihood	-817.5547	Hannan-Quinn criter.	9.434899
F-statistic	10.28838	Durbin-Watson stat	2.357405
Prob(F-statistic)	0.001597		

Source: Researcher's computation (2014)

From the regression result, it was observed that FINEXP with a calculated t-value of 3.20 and a p-value of 0.001 is greater than the critical t-value of 2.0 at 5% level of significance. Therefore, we reject the null hypothesis and accept the alternative hypothesis which states that board members with financial expertise in Nigerian banks have a significant influence on disclosure of information in the annual report.

Hypothesis 5

Ho5. Banks with international subsidiaries whose headquarters are based in Nigeria do not disclose more information than banks with only local branches.

Table 4.16. Test of Hypothesis 5

Variable	Coefficient	Std. Error	t-Statistic	Prob.
C	158.3333	3.022785	52.37995	0.0000
INTSUB	19.00000	3.957754	4.800702	0.0000
R-squared	0.114634	Mean dependent var		147.2500
Adjusted R-squared	0.109660	S.D. dependent var		27.74341
S.E. of regression	26.17809	Akaike info criterion		9.378771
Sum squared resid	121982.0	Schwarz criterion		9.414249
Log likelihood	-842.0894	Hannan-Quinn criter.		9.393156
F-statistic	23.04674	Durbin-Watson stat		2.398575
Prob(F-statistic)	0.000003			

Source: Researcher's computation (2014)

From the regression result, it was observed that INTSUB with a calculated t-value of 4.80 is greater than the critical t-value of 2.0 at 5% level of significance. Therefore, we reject the null hypothesis and accept the alternative hypothesis which states that banks with international subsidiaries whose headquarters are based in Nigeria disclose more information than banks with only local branches.

Hypothesis 6

Ho6. There is no significant positive relationship between the composition of the board of Nigerian banks and the level of disclosure.

Table 4.17. Test of Hypothesis 6

Variable	Coefficient	Std. Error	t-Statistic	Prob.
C	144.2254	2.599519	55.48158	0.0000
BOARDIND	3.529736	1.927690	1.831070	0.0688

R-squared	0.018799	Mean dependent var	147.1017
Adjusted R-squared	0.013192	S.D. dependent var	27.73947
S.E. of regression	27.55589	Akaike info criterion	9.481545
Sum squared resid	132882.3	Schwarz criterion	9.517434
Log likelihood	-837.1167	Hannan-Quinn criter.	9.496100
F-statistic	3.352817	Durbin-Watson stat	0.448631
Prob(F-statistic)	0.068791		

Source: Researcher's computation (2014)

From the regression result, it was observed that BOARDIND with a calculated t-value of 1.8 and a p-value of 0.06 is less than the critical t-value of 2.0 at 5% level of significance. Therefore, we accept the null hypothesis which states that there is no significant positive relationship between the composition of the board of Nigerian banks and the level of disclosure.

CHAPTER FIVE

DISCUSSIONS, CONCLUSIONS AND RECOMMENDATIONS

5.1 Introduction

This study was carried out to critically evaluate the level of disclosure by banks in their annual reports and the key factors that determine the posture of corporate disclosure by bank operators in the Nigerian environment. This chapter begins with a discussion of the key findings and it is followed by a summary of the relevant findings as well as the resultant conclusions. In addition, the chapter further outlines the key policy and general recommendations for further studies. The contributions of this research to the extant body of knowledge are also outlined in this chapter.

5.2 Discussion of Findings

The study showed that there is a significant positive relationship between the total assets of banks in Nigeria and the level of disclosure of the banks. This implies that the larger the size of the banks, the more disclosure the bank would make in its annual report. The findings of this study agree with those of Hossain (2008), Enofe and Isiavwe (2012), Al-Shammari, (2005), Barako, (2007) and Lan, Wang and Zhang (2013). This is because big banks have more shareholders than smaller banks thus they tend to disclose more information. Again, the financial burden of collating and disclosing information is higher on smaller banks than on larger ones. This thereby constricts the level of information gathering and dissemination by the smaller banks. However, the result contradicts Glaum and Street (2003) who found a negative association that is not significantly related to disclosure.

The study also revealed that the age of banks operating in Nigeria has a positive but statistically insignificant relationship with the disclosure posture of banks. This is shown by the results of the Pooled Regression Analysis which gives a t-statistic index of 0.18 for AGE. The findings agree with those of Camfferman and Cooke (2002); Alsaeed (2006); Akhtaruddin (2005); Owusu and Yeoh (2005) and Ansha (1998) as they found a statistically positive association between the level of disclosure and the age of the firm. These authors opined that older banks are more experienced and are therefore, likely to include more information in their annual reports to improve their image and reputation in the market.

This study further revealed that the performance of Nigerian banks has a significant impact on the level of disclosure in their annual reports. This implies that the higher the performance of a bank in terms of profitability, the higher the tendency of the bank to disclose more information. The findings of this study agree with the empirical studies of Enofe and Isiavwe (2012), Owusu-Ansah, (1998), Singhvi and Desai (1971), Hossain (2008) and Karim and Ahmed (2005). All these researchers found a strong positive relationship between bank profitability and disclosure of information.

Also, the results of the random effect model analysed show that there is a positive but statistically insignificant relationship between board independence in Nigerian banks and the level of disclosure. This implies that the presence of more non-executive directors tends to make the boards of banks more effective in terms of reporting but it is not significant. This agrees with the findings of Ho and Wong (2001), Fama and Jensen (1983), Forcker (1992), Lakhal (2004) and Arcay and Vasquez (2005). They showed that a high percentage of non-executive directors on the board increases the control and quality of financial disclosures.

With regard to board members with financial expertise in Nigerian banks, this study found that the number of board members with financial expertise has a significant positive relationship with disclosure of information in the annual report. This implies that boards with more directors with financial expertise are likely to disclose more than banks with few directors with financial expertise on their boards.

The study also found that banks with international subsidiaries whose headquarters are based in Nigeria disclose more information than banks with only local branches. This position agrees with the findings of Raffournier (1995) who studied the extent of disclosure in the annual reports of Swiss listed companies and discovered that internationality plays a major role in the disclosure policy of large firms as internationally diversified companies tend to disclose more information than small purely domestic enterprises. This means that banks with international subsidiaries typically operate across different geographies and cultures with varying disclosure requirements. They are, therefore, likely to have a well built information system that can enable them to track all necessary and essential accounting information for internal and external purposes. It is expected that this will enable them to disclose more accounting information.

5.3 Summary of Findings

Outlined below is the summary of the major findings of the study based on the result of the tested hypotheses.

1. There is a significant positive relationship between the size of banks operating in Nigeria (measured by their total assets) and the level of disclosure of information in their annual reports.
2. The age of banks operating in Nigeria has a positive but not significant impact on the level of disclosure in their annual reports.
3. The performance of Nigerian banks (measured by their profit after tax) has a significant impact on the level of disclosure in their annual reports.
4. The number of board members with financial expertise in Nigerian banks has a significant influence on disclosure of information in the annual reports.

5. Banks with international subsidiaries whose headquarters are based in Nigeria disclose more information than banks with only local branches.

6. The relationship between the composition of the board of Nigerian banks and the level of disclosure is positive but not significant.

5.4 Conclusion

Based on the empirical analysis carried out in this study as well as the results obtained, the following conclusions were arrived at.

1. The major determinants of the level of disclosure by banks in Nigeria are the size of bank operators as measured by their total asset base; the performance of banks as measured by their profitability; presence of international subsidiaries and preponderance of board members with financial expertise. All of these have a positive and significant impact on the disclosure posture of banks operating in Nigeria. Indeed, the bigger the profitability and total assets size of a bank, the more likely it will disclose information to stakeholders. This is generally due to a multiplicity of factors, chief amongst which is the desire of big and profitable banks to signal to stakeholders that they are big, strong and reliable and therefore, can gain the confidence of customers and the investing public both in the short and long term. Also, where the board of a bank is predominantly constituted by persons with financial expertise, greater demands are usually made on the executive management to disclose more information to stakeholders.

2. Factors like the age of a bank and the presence of non-executive directors on the board do not have a significant impact on the disclosure posture of banks operating in Nigeria even though the relationship is positive. This can be attributed to the fact that the banking industry in Nigeria is very highly regulated. Therefore, age and the presence or absence of non-executive directors do not significantly affect disclosure of information to stakeholders.

3. The presence of banks' international subsidiaries expands and broadens the scope of reporting by them. This creates an extra

layer of reporting requirements for banks as stakeholders in different geographies and international settings need to utilize the information provided by the concerned banks in their annual reports.

5.5 Policy Recommendations

Given the fact that corporate disclosure is critical to the functioning of an efficient capital market and the pivotal role that banks play in the entire financial system, every effort must be made to ensure that the disclosure posture of banks is enhanced as much as possible. The following policy recommendations are therefore proffered based on the results of this study.

1. Banks in Nigeria should be encouraged to grow their balance sheet. This will afford them the capacity to finance big ticket transactions and consequently improve their overall profitability and total assets base with the concomitant enhancement of their disclosure posture. The role of the government is critical here as government is required to create an enabling environment that facilitates commerce, wealth creation and promotion of private property rights for individuals. Furthermore, bank regulators are required to come up with innovative steps that would lead to reduced operational costs of doing banking business both for banks and customers for overall enhanced profitability. Such innovative steps could include more profound and widespread shared services for the entire banking industry. This will expectedly enhance the disclosure posture of banks in Nigeria.

2. Concrete steps should be taken to expand the capital base of banks operating in Nigeria to enable them to compete effectively with their counterparts in other geographies both in Africa and in other parts of the world. That way, as shown by the results of this study, they can undoubtedly signal both local and international stakeholders. This is critical as Nigerian banks today are regarded as small players compared to their counterparts in South Africa and the developed countries. For instance, the top 150 biggest banks in Africa are dominated by the "Big Four" South African

banks namely Standard Bank, ABSA, Nedbank and FirstRand Bank (http://www.relbanks.com/worlds-top-banks/assets). Furthermore, the top 50 banks in the world as at March 31, 2014 are from China, United States of America, France, Japan, United Kingdom, Australia, Canada and Germany (http://www.relbanks.com/worlds-top-banks/assets). Therefore, if the level of corporate disclosure in the banking industry is to be enhanced to compare favourably with what obtains in the developed markets, banks in Nigeria should also have the requisite capital base to fund large deals.

3. Based on the results of this study, it is imperative that banks operating in Nigeria have boards which are significantly comprised of directors with financial expertise. This will, undoubtedly, engender a regime of enhanced disclosure as the directors will bring to bear the requisite skills and knowledge that they have in the conduct of their oversight functions in their respective banks. The Central Bank is thus encouraged to review the criteria for board membership by bank directors and raise the bar to ensure that only duly qualified persons are considered eligible for membership of the boards of banks based on a fairly rigorous set of eligibility criteria that incorporate clear ingredients of financial expertise.

4. There is the need for boards of directors of banks to undergo constant training and retraining especially on financial matters in order to enhance their level of financial expertise. In this regard, it is hereby recommended that all boards of banks should undergo at least two training sessions per annum. Such sessions should incorporate various aspects of financial management required to improve their oversight of banks. The Chartered Institute of Bankers in Nigeria (CIBN) should champion this initiative and work closely with the Bank Directors Association of Nigeria (BDAN). Also, there should be a mandatory annual continuing education requirement for bank directors which should be religiously monitored by the CIBN.

5. Based on the fact that there is a significant positive correlation between international subsidiaries and the disclosure posture of banks, it is hereby recommended that banks should be encouraged

to open international subsidiaries with a view to expanding their scope of operations and thus further enhance their disclosure posture. This should, however, be done after a carefully thought out business case is done for each country or location.

5.6 Recommendations for Future Research

This study evaluated the determinants of corporate disclosure by banks that operate in Nigeria using a disclosure index that was developed taking into cognizance all the disclosure variables that pertain to the Nigerian banking environment as well as international disclosure requirements. Available data were obtained and analysed in the study and significant conclusions were reached. However, future investigations in this field of study may wish to consider other areas which were excluded so as to gain greater insight. These are outlined below.

i. The study considered only the Deposit Money Banks (DMBs) as listed by the Central Bank of Nigeria. Further studies can expand the scope to include other institutions in the financial services space, like Microfinance Banks (MFBs), Primary Mortgage Institutions (PMIs), and Discount Houses (DHs). This will provide a bigger picture of the corporate disclosure posture of organizations that operate within the financial services industry.

ii. A targeted research could be conducted in the future purely for Bureau De Change (BDC) operators. This is necessary given the fairly narrow scope of operation of BDC entities in Nigeria.

iii. Future researchers could also expand the scope of the study to cover all listed companies on the Nigerian Stock Exchange. This will throw more light on the overall disclosure posture of quoted companies in Nigeria.

iv. Another critical area that future researchers could look at is the time period of the study. This current study covered a period of nine years, from 2005 – 2013. Future studies could expand the time period to cover up to 10, 15 or 20 years for greater insight.

v. During the course of conducting this research, the non-interest bearing bank in Nigeria, Jaiz Bank, was excluded due to lack of comparable data as it does not provide conventional commercial banking services. Furthermore, it only commenced operation in the year 2012. It is expected that future research studies could also focus on non interest banks in the country to gain greater insight into the disclosure posture of non-interest banks in Nigeria.

5.7 Contributions to Knowledge

Based on the rigorous empirical nature of this study, the timeliness thereof and the results derived, the following can be considered as the key contributions to knowledge.

i.   The study focused on evaluating the determinants of corporate disclosure in the banking industry in Nigeria using six key variables. From available records, this is the first empirical research work in this area that used these variables to evaluate the disclosure posture of banks in Nigeria. The unique results and recommendations flowing from the study are an indubitable contribution to knowledge.

ii. As part of conducting the study, a disclosure index was designed containing two hundred and nineteen (219) disclosure items. This index took cognizance of all the corporate disclosure requirements in Nigeria including the IFRS requirements. This is regarded as epochal and a unique contribution to knowledge as there is no known empirical study that comprehensively designed such an index that is tailored to the Nigerian environment for the purpose of evaluating the disclosure posture of Nigerian banks.

iii. This study provides a veritable basis or framework which can be used as a guide for the purpose of designing new policies for the regulation of banks in Nigeria especially in relation to minimum capital requirements and cost efficiency measures for enhanced profitability and sustainability with the concomitant enhancement of disclosure by banks.

REFERENCES

Abiola, J.O. & Ojo, S.O. (2012). Compliance with regulatory financial reporting and corporate governance practices in selected primary mortgage institutions in Nigeria. *International Journal of Business and Social Science 3 (15)*; 246-254.

Adeyemi, S. B. & Fagbemi, T. O. (2010). Audit quality, corporate governance and firm characteristics in Nigeria. *International Journal of Business and Management.* 5 (5). 169-179

Adina, P. & Ion, P. (2008) Aspects regarding corporate mandatory and voluntary Disclosure Retrieved from: http://steconomice.uoradea.ro/anale/volume/2008/v3-finances-banks-accountancy/256.pdf on 5th July 2012.

Ainofenokhai, J. (2014) Rebased GDP, World Bank and Nigeria's realities. *Vanguard.* April 13, 2014. Retrieved from: http://www.vanguardngr.com/2014/04/rebased-gdp-world-bank-nigerias-realities/

Ajakaiye, O. & Olowookere, A. (2013). Financial inclusion in Nigeria. Paper presented at the 18th Central Bank of Nigeria (CBN) seminar for finance correspondents and business editors at Umuahia, Abia State. Retrieved from: http://www. mydailynewswatchng.com/2013/07/07/financial-inclusion-in-nigeria/ on 10th September 2013.

Akhtaruddin, M. (2005). Corporate mandatory disclosure practices in Bangladesh. *International Journal of Accounting,* 40, 399- 422.

Alsaeed, K. (2006). The association between firm-specific characteristics and disclosure: The case of Saudi Arabia. *Managerial Auditing Journal, 21*(5), 476 - 496

Al-Shammari, B.A. (2005). Compliance with IAS by listed companies in the gulf co-operation member states: an empirical study. Unpublished doctoral dissertation, University of Western Australia, Perth.

Amihud, Y. & Mendelson, H. (1986) Asset pricing and the bid-ask spread. *Journal of Financial Economics 17*: 223–49.

Ansah. (1998).The impact of corporate attributes on the extent of mandatory disclosure and reporting by listed companies in Zimbabwe. *The international journal of accounting, 33*(1), 605-631.

Anyanwu, E. O. & Ogbonna, A. (2011). Recapitalization: controversy over planned sale of Afribank. Daily Sun. April 04, 2011. Nigeria.

Atuanya, P. & Augie, B. (2014). Breaking down Nigeria rebased $510 billion GDP. *Business Day* April 7, 2014. Retrieved from: http://businessdayonline. com/2014/04 /breaking-down- nigeria - rebased-510-billion-gdp/

Awotundun, D. A & Kehinde, J. S. (2011). Corporate governance and stakeholders interest: A case study of Nigerian banks. *International Journal of Business and Management*. 6 (10); October 2011. Retrieved from: http:// dx.doi.org/10.5539/ijbm.v6n10p102

Baker, H. & Anderson, R. (2010). *Corporate governance: A synthesis of theory, research, and practice.* New Jersey. John Wiley & Sons, Inc.

Barako, D. G. (2007). Determinants of voluntary disclosures in Kenyan companies annual reports. *African Journal of Business Management, 1 (5),* 113-128.

Barako, D; Hancock, P. & Izan, H. (2006). Relationship between corporate governance attributes and voluntary disclosures in annual reports: The Kenyan experience. *Financial Reporting, Regulation and Governance. 5(1)*; 1-25.

Bhasin, M.L. (2010). Corporate governance disclosure practices: The portrait of a developing country. *International Journal of Business and Management.* 5 (4).

Bushman, R. & Smith, A. (2003) Transparency, financial accounting information and Corporate governance. Retrieved from: http://public. kenan-flagler.unc.edu/faculty/bushmanr/202rbus.pdf on 5th july 2012.

Cadbury Code. (1992). The report of the committee on the financial aspects of corporate governance: The code of best practices. London. Gee professional publishing.

Camfferman, K. & Cooke, T. E. (2002). An analysis of disclosure in the annual reports of U.K. And Dutch companies. *Journal of International Accounting Research, 1*,3-30.

Central Bank of Nigeria – CBN, (2013). CBN designates eight banks 'too big to fail'. Thisday Live. 12 Nov 2013. Retrieved from: http://www.thisdaylive. com/articles /cbn-designates-eight-banks-too-big-to-fail-/164074/

Central Bank of Nigeria – CBN, (2013). Financial institutions. Retrieved from http://www.cenbank. org/ Supervision /finstitutions.asp.

Central Bank of Nigeria – CBN, (2014). List of financial institutions. Retrieved from: www.ecgi.org/**codes**/documents/cg **code** nigeria 16may**2014** en.pdf

Collett P., and Hrasky S. (2005). Voluntary disclosure of corporate governance practices by listed Australian companies. *Journal of Corporate Governance: An International Review, 13 (2)*,188-196.

Cooke, T.E. (1992). The impact of size, stock market listing and industry type on disclosure in the annual reports of Japanese listed corporations. *Accounting and Business Research, 22* (87), 229 -237.

Consulate General of Nigeria, Hong Kong (2013). The structure of the Nigerian financial system. Retrieved From: http://www.nigeria-consulate.

org.hk/ Common/Reader/Channel /ShowPage.jsp? Cid=5&Pid
=4&Version=0&Charset=iso-8859-1&page=0.

Dabor, E. L. & Adeyemi, S. B. (2009). Corporate governance and the
credibility of financial statements in Nigeria. *Journal of Business Systems,
Governance and Ethics. 4 (1)*. 13 – 24.

Dey, A. (2005). Corporate governance and financial reporting
credibility. ProQuest® dissertations & theses. Retrieved from: http://
gateway.proquest.com/openurl%3furl ver=Z39.88-2004%26res
dat=xri:pqdiss%26rft val fmt=info:ofi/fmt:kev:mtx:dissertation%
n26rft dat=xri:pqdiss:3177709 on 10th January 2012

Digital Africa (2013). How mobile banking can promote financial inclusion
in Nigeria. Retrieved from: http://www.digitalafrica.com.ng/?p=147 on 7th
December 2013.

DisclosureNet (2012) Corporate disclosure. Retrieved From: http://
www.slideshare.net / davidisiavwe / savedfiles?s_title =what-is-corporate-
disclosure&user_login= DisclosureNet

Donaldson, L. & Davis, J. (1991). Stewardship theory or agency theory:
Ceo governance and shareholder returns. *Australian Journal of Management,
16 (1)*. 49 – 65.

Eisenhardt, M, K. (1989). Agency theory: An assessment and review.
Academy of Management Review, 14 (1), 57-74.

Enhancing Financial Innovation & Access - EFInA (2013). EFInA Quarterly
Review (Apr-Jun 2013). 5. Retrieved from: http://217.198.108.236/
publications/ market-reviews/

Enofe, A. & Isiavwe, D. (2012). Corporate disclosure and governance in
the Nigerian banking sector: An empirical evaluation. *The International
Journal's Research Journal of Social Science & Management. Singapore*. ISSN:
2251-1571. Retrieved From: Website: www.tij.sg

Ernst & Young, Australia (2009). "Non financial reporting". Retrieved From: http://www.ey.com /Publication/vwLUAssets/Non-financial _ Federal Republic of Nigeria. Banks and other Financial Institutions Act. Chapter b 3, volume 2. The laws of the Federation of Nigeria 2004.

Gernon, L. & Meek, G. (2001) *Accounting: An international perspective.* New York. Irwin McGraw – Hill.

Glaum, M. & Street, D. (2003). Compliance with the disclosure requirement of German's new market, IAS Versus US GAAP. *Journal of International Financial Management and Accounting, 14(1)*, 64-100.

Glautier, M; Underdown, B. & Morris, D. (2011). *Accounting theory and practice.* Great Britain. Pearson Education Limited.

Glosten, L. & Milgrom, P. (1985) Bid, ask, and transaction prices in a specialist market with heterogeneously informed traders. *Journal of Financial Economics* 14: 71–100.

Gu, F. & Li, J. (2007). The credibility of voluntary disclosure and insider stock transactions. Journal of Accounting Research. 45 (4) 771 – 810.

Healy, P. M. & Palepu, K. G. (2001) Information asymmetry, corporate disclosure, and the capital markets: a review of the empirical disclosure literature. Journal of Accounting and Economics 31 (2001) 405–440.

Heidhues, E & Patel, C (2010) IFRS and exercise of accountants' professional judgments: Insights and concerns from a German perspective. Retreived From: http://www.researchgate.net/publication/ 228429841_IFRS_and_exercise_of_accountants'_professional_ judgments_ Insights_and_concerns_from_a_German_perspective

Hossain, M. (2008). The extent of disclosure in annual reports of banking companies: The case Of India. European Journal of Scientific Research 23(4).659-680. Retrieved From: http://www.eurojournals. com/ejsr.htm.

International Federation of Accountants - IFAC (2003). Establishing credibility in the investor community. http://www.ifac.org/sites /default/ files/ publications /files/3.1- Carlos - Madrazo-.Madrazo-establishing-credibility-final.pdf.

International Monetary Fund (2013). Nigeria: 2012 article iv consultation--staff report; IMF country report 13/116. Retrieved From:http://www.imf.org/external/pubs/ft/scr/2013/cr13116.pdf

Investopedia (2013). Disclosure. http://www.investopedia.com/terms/d/disclosure.asp

Jensen, M.C. & Meckling, W. H. (1976). Theory of the firm: Managerial behavior, agency costs, and ownership structure. *Journal of Financial Economics*, 3, 305–360.

Kam, V. (1990). *Accounting Theory*. (2nd Edition). New York. John Wiley & Sons.

Karim, W. A. & Ahmed, U. J. (2005). Determinants of IAS disclosure compliance in emerging economies: Evidence from exchange listed companies in Bangladesh. Working paper series. Working paper no. 21 2005. Retrieved from: https://www.victoria.ac. nz /sacl/centres –and -institutes/ cagtr/working-papers/WP21.pdf

Kiel, G.C. & Gavin, J.N. (2003). Board composition and corporate performance: How the Australian experience informs contrasting theories of corporate governance. *Corporate Governance: An International Review. 11(3)*, 189-205.

Lan, Y; Wang, L; & Zhang, X (2013). Determinants and features of voluntary disclosure in the Chinese stock market. *China Journal of Accounting Research 6 (2013) 265–285*. Retrieved from: journal homepage: www.elsevier.com/locate/cjar

Lee, P; Stokes, D; Taylor, S; & Walter, T. (2003). The association between audit quality, accounting disclosures and firm-specific risk: Evidence from initial public offerings. *Journal of Accounting and Public Policy* 22 (2003) 377–400 379.

Mendes-Da-Silva, W. & Christensen, T. (2004). Determinants of voluntary disclosure of financial information on the internet by Brazilian firms. Retrieved from: http://dx.doi.org/10.2139/ssrn.638082

McRitchie (2013). Corporate governance defined. corporate governance. Retrieved from: http://corpgov.net/2013/10/corporate-governance-stepping-back-in- time-from-october-2013/

Merton, R. (1987). A simple model of capital market equilibrium with incomplete information. *Journal of Finance* 42: 483–510.

Muhamad, R; Shahimi, S; Yahya, Y; & Mahzan, N; (2009). Disclosure quality on governance issues in annual reports of malaysian plcs. International Business Research. 2 (4). 61-72.

Naser, K. & Nuseibeh, R. (2003). Quality of financial reporting: Evidence from the listed saudi non-financial companies. *The International Journal of Accounting*, 38 (1), 41-70.

Needles, B. E. (1997). International accounting research: an analysis of thirty-two years from the international journal of accounting. *The International Journal of Accounting*, 32, 203-235.

Nworji, D; Olagunju, A. & Adeyanju, D. (2011). Corporate governance and bank failure In Nigeria: Issues, challenges and opportunities. *Research Journal of Finance and Accounting*. 2 (2), 2011.

Ogubunka, U. M. (2003). *Walking ahead of bank distress - the secret of safeguarding your money in banks. a practical guide*. Lagos. Rhema Enterprises.

Ogujiuba, K. & Obiechina, M. (2011). Financial sector reforms in Nigeria: Issues and challenges. *International Journal of Business and Management*. 6 (6): 222.

Okeahalam, C. C. & Akinboade, O. A. (2003). A review of corporate governance in Africa: Literature, issues and challenges, Washington. *Global Corporate Governance Forum.*

Okoye, A.E. (1996). The impact of price level changes on accounting information in a depressed economy. *The National Accountant.* January 1996. Pp 9-12

Okoye, A.E. (2000). *Financial accounting for students and managers.* Benin City, Nigeria. Mindex Publishing Co. Ltd.

Organization for Economic Cooperation and Development – OECD (2004). OECD principles Of corporate governance, Paris France. OECD Publications Service.

Osazee, B.E. & Izedonmi, P.F. (2008). Guidelines for writing theses & dissertations for postgraduate students in Africa. Lagos, Nigeria. Streams Communications.

Owusu-Ansah, S. & Yeoh, J. (2005). The effect of legislation on corporate disclosure practices. *ABACUS, 41* (1), 92 –109.

Prani, J. (2005) The history of Nigeria banking system. Retrieved from: http://answers.yahoo.com/question/index?qid=1006052015333

Raffournier, B. (1995). The determinants of voluntary financial disclosure by Swiss listed companies. *European Accounting Review Volume 4, Issue 2, 261-280.*

Rahman, S. (2012). Impression management motivations, strategies and disclosure credibility of corporate narratives. *Journal Of Management Research.* 4 (3).

Randle, J. K. (2012) Freedom of misinformation: trouble in the air. Business Day NewsPapers. http://www.businessdayonline.com/

Rezaee, Z. (2009). The role of internal auditors in corporate governance, paper Presented at the PhD colloquium organized by Faculty of Business and Accountancy, 4 June, Kuala Lumpur.

Ridwan, K. (2011) The banking industry in the last fifty years. Nigerian commentaries Retrieved from: http://nigeriancommentaries.blogspot. com/2011/02/banking-industry-in-last-fifty-years.html on 10th January 2012

Sambo, I. L. (2011). Business: Securities fraud. http://trifter.com/africa / nigeria/business -securities-fraud/ on 10th January 2012.

Sanusi, L. S. (2012) Banking reform and its impact on the Nigerian economy. Being a Lecture delivered at the University of Warwick's Economic Summit, UK 17th February, 2012. Retrieved from: http://www. cenbank.org/out/speeches/2012/gov _ warwick _150211.pdf

Shaibu, I. I. (2012). *Introduction to applied research and economics.* Benin City. ACME Publishers.

Singhvi, S. S., & Desai, H. B. (1971). An empirical analysis of quality of corporate Financial disclosure. *The Accounting Review,* January, 129-138.

Ştefănescu, C. A. (2012). Corporate governance disclosure – an international overview of research trends. *Economics and Management:* 17 (3).

The library of congress country studies; CIA World Fact book (1991). Nigeria banking, finance, and other services. Retrieved from: http://www.photius. com/countries/nigeria/ economy /nigeria economy banking finance an-10016.html

Turrent, G. (2012) Corporate information transparency on the internet by listed companies in Spain (IBEX35) and Mexico (IPYC). *Retrieved from: http://www.readperiodicals. com/201201 / 2643855661.html#ixzz1 xAaekmD5*

Uyar, A. & Kilic, M. (2012). Influence of corporate attributes on forward-looking Information disclosure in publicly traded Turkish corporations. *Procedia - Social and Behavioral Sciences. Elsevier Ltd. Sele.* 62: 244 – 252

Vintilă, G. & Gherghina, S. (2012) An empirical examination of the relationship between corporate governance ratings and listed companies' performance. *International Journal of Business and Management*, 7 (22); 46-61.

World Bank (2012). Global financial development report 2013: Rethinking the role of the state in finance. Washington, DC: doi:10.1596/978-0-8213-9503-5.

Yusoff, W. F. & Alhaji, I. A. (2012). Insight of corporate governance theories. *Journal of Business &Management*. Article ID:2012-12-01-52. Retrieved From: https://www.academia.edu/2381859/Insight_of_Corporate_Governance_Theories.

A P P E N D I C E S

Appendix I
List of Banks Reviewed

1	Access Bank Plc
2	Citibank Nigeria Limited
3	Diamond Bank Plc
4	Ecobank Nigeria Plc
5	Wema Bank Plc
6	Fidelity Bank Plc
7	First Bank of Nigeria Plc
8	First City Monument Bank Plc
9	Guaranty Trust Bank Plc
10	Zenith Bank Plc
11	Key Stone Bank
12	MainStreet Bank
13	Skye Bank Plc
14	Stanbic IBTC Bank Ltd.
15	Standard Chartered Bank Nigeria Ltd.
16	Sterling Bank Plc
17	Union Bank of Nigeria Plc
18	United Bank For Africa Plc
19	Unity Bank Plc

Appendix II
Disclosure Index (mandatory items)

A. Balance Sheet/Statement of Financial Position Items (20)

1	1. Share Capital and share premium with their related note
2	2. Retained earnings with the related note
3	3. Other Reserves with the related note
4	4. Borrowings and the related note
5	5. Income tax liabilities and the related note
6	6. Post employment benefits and the related note
7	7. Deposits from banks and the related note
8	8. Deposits from customers and the related note
9	9. Other liabilities and provision and the related note
10	10. Cash and cash equivalents with the related note
11	11. Trading assets with the related note
12	12. Pledged assets with the related note
13	13. Investment securities and the related note
14	14. Loans and Advances and the related note
15	15. Investment in equity accounted investee and the related note
16	16. Investment in subsidiaries and the related note
17	17. Property and equipment and the related note
18	18. Intangible assets and the related note
19	19. Deferred tax assets and liabilities and the related note
20	20. Other assets and the related note

B. Profit and Loss Account/Statement of Comprehensive Income Items (12)

21	1. Interest income and the related note
22	2. Fee and commission income and the related note
23	3. Trading income and the related note
24	4. Other income and the related note
25	5. Interest expense and the related note

C. Statement of Changes in Equity (03)

D. Cash Flow Statement (03)

E. Board Report (14) – *Section 342 of CAMA*

F. Corporate Governance (10):

G. General Risk Management (07):

H. Credit Risk Exposure (11):

70   1. Disclosure on the magnitude of an institution's credit exposure on an aggregate basis

71   2. Information on credit risk management structure

72   3. Quantitative information on gross loan positions

73   4. Disclosures about the quality of the current loan and other counter-party exposures with quantitative information

74   5. Amount and details of problem loans and other assets or details by internal risk ratings

75   6. Disclosure of credit rating system/process

76   7. Ageing schedule of past due loans and advances (NPLs)

77   8. Credit concentration by industry

78   9. Credit concentration by location

79   10. Credit quality disclosures

80   11. Disclosure about risk management process (use of risk-mitigating tools such as collaterals, guarantees, netting agreement, managing concentrations)

I. Market Risk Exposure (04):

81   1. General descriptions of market risk segments

82   2. Disclosures on value-at-risk (VAR) for interest rate exposure

83   3. Disclosures on value-at-risk (VAR) for foreign exchange exposure

84   4. Disclosures on value-at-risk (VAR) for trading and derivatives securities exposure

J. Interest Rate Risk (03):

85   1. Detailed quantitative information about the nature and extent of interest rate-sensitive assets, liabilities and off-balance sheet exposures including;

86   2. Averages

87   3. Breakdown of fixed and floating rate items for liabilities and assets

K. Currency Risk (03):

L. Liquidity Risk Exposure (03):

M. Other Information (16):

Disclosure Index (Voluntary Items)

A. Background about the bank/general corporate information (06):

110	1. Brief narrative history of the Bank
111	2. Basic organization structure/chart/description of corporate structure
112	3. General description of business activities
113	4. Date of establishment
114	5. Official address/registered address/address for correspondence
115	6. Web address of the bank/email address

B. Corporate Strategy (03):

116	1. Management's objectives and strategies/corporate vision/ motto/statement of corporate goals or objectives
117	2. Future strategy - Information of future expansion (capital expenditures)/general development of business
118	3. Impact of strategy on future results

C. Corporate Governance (21):

119	1. Details about the chairman including name/title/background of the chairman/academic/professional/business experiences
120	2. Details about directors including name/title/background of the directors/ academic/professional/business experiences
121	3. List of senior managers (not on the board of directors)/senior management structure
122	4. Background of senior managers
123	5. Details of CEO's contact address
124	6. Are the independent directors well-defined?
125	7. Directors' engagement/directorship of other companies
126	8. Photographs of all directors/Board Members
127	9. Disclosure on management succession plan.

128	10. Disclosure on code of conduct/ethics for Directors, Management and staff.
129	11. Disclosure of Govt direct and indirect equity holding in the bank (limited to 10% by end of 2007).
130	12. Disclosure on CEO Duality i.e. CEO is different from the Chairman.
131	13. Disclosure that no two members of the same extended family occupy the position of Chairman and that of Chief Executive Officer or Executive Director of a bank at the same time.
132	14. Disclosure of annual training and education of board members
133	15. Disclosure of presence of independent directors on the board
134	16. Disclosure of tenor of non-executive directors - maximum of 3 terms of 4 years each, i.e. 12 years.
135	17. Disclosure that Board Chairman does not serve as chairman/member of any of the board committees
136	18. Disclosure of annual Board and Directors' review/appraisal by an outside consultant.
137	19. Disclosure of tenor of external auditors (maximum 10 years)
138	20. Disclosure that a bank's external auditors do not provide other services such as book-keeping, Internal Audit outsourcing, HR functions, etc that can compromise their position.
139	21. Disclosure on periodic "peer review" of compensation and remuneration levels to ensure competitiveness

D. Industry Transparency, Due Process, Data Integrity and Disclosure Requirements (04):

| 140 | 1. Disclosure of existence of 'whistle blowing' policy/procedures that encourage reporting of unethical behavior. |
| 141 | 2. Disclosure of corporate governance compliance status in the audited financial statements. |

142	3. Disclosure on plans/strategy for managing the impact of HIV/AIDS, Malaria and other serious diseases on company's employees and their families.
143	4. Disclosure of special examination carried out by the CBN on the Bank during the financial year.

E. Financial Performance (13):

144	1. Brief discussion and analysis of a bank's financial position
145	2. Discussion of the bank's liquidity position and about additional financing
146	3. Qualitative forecast of earnings
147	4. Return on equity
148	**5.** Net interest margin
149	6. Cost–to-income ratio
150	7. Earnings per share
151	8. Risk-weighted assets
152	9. Debt–to-equity ratio
153	10. Total liquid assets to assets ratio
154	11. Total liquid assets to deposit ratio
155	12. Loan to deposit ratio
156	13. Dividend per share

F. Accounting Policy Review (02):

157	1. Discussion on its accounting policy
158	2. Disclosure of accounting standards used for its accounts

G. Key Non-financial Statistics (08):

159	1. Age of key employees
160	2. Details of branch location
161	3. Number of branches
162	4. No. of branch expansion during the financial year

163	5. Information on branch computerization
164	6. Information on ATMs
165	7. Location of ATMs and their addresses
166	8. List of top five shareholders of the bank

H. Corporate Social Disclosure (03):

167	1. Sponsoring public health, sporting of recreational projects
168	2. Supporting national pride/government.-sponsored campaigns
169	3. Information on social banking activities/banking for the society

I. Others (50):

170	1. Chairman's/MD's report
171	2. Disclosure of on-line banking facilities/ E-Business innovation
172	3. Information on cards business
173	4. Information on international banking facilities
174	5. Information on international Subsidiaries
175	6. Information on ISO (and other) certifications
176	**7.** Graphical presentation of performance indicators
177	8. Information regarding remuneration of committee members
178	9. Information on remuneration of directors/MD-CEO
179	10. Name of the director heading the shareholders' grievance committee
180	11. Name and designation of compliance officer
181	12. Number of shareholders' complaints received so far
182	13. Number of shareholders' complaints not solved to the satisfaction of shareholders
183	14. Number of pending complaints
184	15. Disclosure of materially significant related party transactions
185	16. Disclosure of accounting treatment

APPENDIX III
Detailed Analysis Results (E-views 8.0)

	DISINDEX	TASSETS	AGE	PAT	FINEXP	INTSUB	BOARDIND
Mean	146.4444	1.59E+09	26.33918	3.83E+09	12.90643	0.578947	0.822800
Median	137.0000	6.02E+08	21.00000	17077918	6.000000	1.000000	0.625000
Maximum	197.0000	3.12E+10	119.0000	9.58E+10	75.00000	1.000000	6.500000
Minimum	166.0000	25229804	13.00000	-13940985	0.000000	0.000000	0.142857
Std. Dev.	27.41492	3.61E+09	15.86901	1.56E+10	17.35723	0.495178	1.095494
Skewness	-0.075195	5.893731	2.979647	4.742996	2.144336	-0.319801	4.908905
Kurtosis	2.162582	43.29036	12.78658	24.89855	6.566654	1.102273	25.61383
Jarque–Bera	5.157694	12556.08	935.4432	4057.904	221.6853	28.57453	4330.395
Probability	0.075861	0.000000	0.000000	0.000000	0.000000	0.000001	0.000000
Sum	25042.00	2.72E+11	4504.000	6.56E+11	2207.000	99.00000	140.6989
Sum Sq. Dev.	127768.2	2.21E+21	42810.33	4.16E+22	51216.50	41.68421	204.0183
Observations	171	171	171	171	171	171	171

Covariance Analysis: Ordinary
Date: 10/02/14 Time: 16:57
Sample: 1 180
Included observations: 171
Balanced sample (listwise missing value deletion)

Correlation t-Statistic Probability	DISINDEX	TASSETS	AGE	PAT	FINEXP	INTSUB	BOARDIND
DISINDEX	1.000000						

TASSETS	0.165490	1.000000					
	2.181445	-----					
	0.0305	-----					
AGE	0.045001	0.245637	1.000000				
	0.585612	3.294205	-----				
	0.5589	0.0012	-----				
PAT	0.226912	0.039994	0.091734	1.000000			
	3.028859	0.520333	1.197591	-----			
	0.0028	0.6035	0.2328	-----			
FINEXP	0.242961	0.164248	0.340232	0.095731	1.000000		
	3.256061	2.164627	4.703631	1.250249	-----		
	0.0014	0.0318	0.0000	0.2129	-----		
INTSUB	0.373950	0.130738	0.200187	0.207215	-0.227040	1.000000	
	5.241637	1.714310	2.656196	2.753564	3.030669	-----	
	0.0000	0.0883	0.0087	0.0065	0.0028	-----	
BOARDIND	0.145980	0.013275	0.003556	0.053646	0.224475	0.237789	1.000000
	1.918286	0.172592	0.046229	0.698402	2.994600	3.182546	-----
	0.0568	0.8632	0.9632	0.4859	0.0032	0.0017	-----

Dependent Variable: DISINDEX
Method: Least Squares
Date: 10/02/14 Time: 17:01
Sample: 1 180
Included observations: 171

Variable	Coefficient	Std. Error	t-Statistic	Prob.
C	152.3518	4.467028	34.10584	0.0000
TASSETS	1.48E-09	5.46E-10	2.717113	0.0073
AGE	0.025662	0.135585	0.189267	0.8501
PAT	2.65E-10	1.25E-10	2.127193	0.0349
FINEXP	0.311444	0.124800	2.495308	0.0327
INTSUB	18.73239	4.294701	4.361745	0.0000
BOARDIND	0.904986	1.801648	0.502310	0.6161

R-squared	0.424917	Mean dependent var		146.4444
Adjusted R-squared	0.396560	S.D. dependent var		27.41492
S.E. of regression	24.57331	Akaike info criterion		9.281273
Sum squared resid	99030.99	Schwarz criterion		9.409879
Log likelihood	-786.5488	Hannan-Quinn criter.		9.333456
F-statistic	7.931702	Durbin-Watson stat		1.662536
Prob(F-statistic)	0.000000			

DIAGNOSTICS

Variance Inflation Factors
Date: 10/02/14 Time: 17:02
Sample: 1 180
Included observations: 171

Variable	Coefficient Variance	Uncentered VIF	Centered VIF
C	19.95434	5.650752	NA
TASSETS	2.98E-19	1.305252	1.091086
AGE	0.018383	4.914849	1.303293
PAT	1.55E-20	1.132321	1.067741
FINEXP	0.015575	2.055729	1.321028
INTSUB	18.44446	3.023945	1.273240
BOARDIND	3.245936	1.718981	1.096685

Breusch-Godfrey Serial Correlation LM Test:

F-statistic	119.8229	Prob. F(2,162)	0.3544
Obs*R-squared	102.0288	Prob. Chi-Square(2)	0.3423

Test Equation:
Dependent Variable: RESID
Method: Least Squares
Date: 10/02/14 Time: 17:02
Sample: 1 180
Included observations: 171
Presample and interior missing value lagged residuals set to zero.

Variable	Coefficient	Std. Error	t-Statistic	Prob.
C	0.106954	2.854493	0.037469	0.9702
TASSETS	-1.54E-10	3.49E-10	-0.442078	0.6590
AGE	0.014410	0.086656	0.166287	0.8681
PAT	1.19E-10	8.04E-11	1.484627	0.1396
FINEXP	0.037930	0.079843	0.475052	0.6354
INTSUB	-0.948995	2.746938	-0.345474	0.7302
BOARDIND	-0.569206	1.152221	-0.494008	0.6220
RESID(-1)	0.759233	0.075630	10.03873	0.0000
RESID(-2)	0.038964	0.077432	0.503203	0.6155

R-squared	0.596659	Mean dependent var	-6.23E-15
Adjusted R-squared	0.576741	S.D. dependent var	24.13577
S.E. of regression	15.70233	Akaike info criterion	8.396691
Sum squared resid	39943.21	Schwarz criterion	8.562041
Log likelihood	-708.9171	Hannan-Quinn criter.	8.463783
F-statistic	29.95572	Durbin-Watson stat	1.898691
Prob(F-statistic)	0.000000		

Heteroskedasticity Test: Breusch-Pagan-Godfrey

F-statistic	5.186574	Prob. F(6,164)	0.4561
Obs*R-squared	27.27266	Prob. Chi-Square(6)	0.4324
Scaled explained SS	16.40054	Prob. Chi-Square(6)	0.4118

Test Equation:
Dependent Variable: RESID^2
Method: Least Squares
Date: 10/02/14 Time: 17:03
Sample: 1 180
Included observations: 171

Variable	Coefficient	Std. Error	t-Statistic	Prob.
C	946.9391	112.6965	8.402559	0.0000
TASSETS	-2.22E-08	1.38E-08	-1.614673	0.1083
AGE	-0.643224	3.420600	-0.188044	0.8511
PAT	7.20E-09	3.14E-09	2.289772	0.0233
FINEXP	-10.16475	3.148520	-3.228420	0.0015
INTSUB	-305.9670	108.3490	-2.823903	0.0053
BOARDIND	-42.17330	45.45292	-0.927846	0.3549

R-squared	0.159489	Mean dependent var	579.1286
Adjusted R-squared	0.128739	S.D. dependent var	664.1731
S.E. of regression	619.9483	Akaike info criterion	15.73722
Sum squared resid	63031079	Schwarz criterion	15.86583
Log likelihood	-1338.533	Hannan-Quinn criter.	15.78941
F-statistic	5.186574	Durbin-Watson stat	0.857084
Prob(F-statistic)	0.000065		

PANEL

Dependent Variable: DISINDEX
Method: Panel EGLS (Period random effects)
Date: 10/02/14 Time: 17:12
Sample: 2005 2013
Periods included: 9
Cross-sections included: 20
Total panel (unbalanced) observations: 171
Swamy and Arora estimator of component variances

Variable	Coefficient	Std. Error	t-Statistic	Prob.
C	152.3518	4.554199	33.45303	0.0000
TASSETS	1.48E-09	5.57E-10	2.665106	0.0085
AGE	0.025662	0.138230	0.185644	0.8530
PAT	2.65E-10	1.27E-10	2.086477	0.0385
FINEXP	0.168144	0.127235	1.321519	0.1882
INTSUB	18.73239	4.378509	4.278258	0.0000
BOARDIND	0.904986	1.836806	0.492696	0.6229

Effects Specification

			S.D.	Rho
Period random			0.000000	0.0000
Idiosyncratic random			25.05284	1.0000

Weighted Statistics

R-squared	0.224917	Mean dependent var	146.4444
Adjusted R-squared	0.196560	S.D. dependent var	27.41492
S.E. of regression	24.57331	Sum squared resid	99030.99
F-statistic	7.931702	Durbin-Watson stat	0.462536
Prob(F-statistic)	0.000000		

Un-weighted Statistics

R-squared	0.224917	Mean dependent var	146.4444
Sum squared resid	99030.99	Durbin-Watson stat	0.462536

Correlated Random Effects - Hausman Test

Equation: Untitled

Test period random effects

Test Summary	Chi-Sq. Statistic	Chi-Sq. d.f.	Prob.
Period random	1.611968	6	0.9517

** WARNING: estimated period random effects variance is zero.

Period random effects test comparisons:

Variable	Fixed	Random	Var(Diff.)	Prob.
TASSETS	0.000000	0.000000	0.000000	0.3953
AGE	-0.010975	0.025662	0.001477	0.3404
PAT	-0.000000	-0.000000	0.000000	0.5529
FINEXP	0.171326	0.168144	0.000092	0.7407
INTSUB	-18.334027	-18.732390	0.348042	0.4995
BOARDIND	0.901995	0.904986	0.142515	0.9937

Period random effects test equation:
Dependent Variable: DISINDEX
Method: Panel Least Squares
Date: 10/02/14 Time: 17:13
Sample: 2005 2013
Periods included: 9
Cross-sections included: 20
Total panel (unbalanced) observations: 171

Variable	Coefficient	Std. Error	t-Statistic	Prob.
C	153.2300	4.665494	32.84324	0.0000
TASSETS	1.41E-09	5.64E-10	2.495009	0.0136
AGE	0.010975	0.143472	0.076494	0.9391
PAT	2.81E-10	1.30E-10	2.163780	0.0320
FINEXP	0.171326	0.127598	1.342699	0.1813
INTSUB	18.33403	4.418075	4.149778	0.0001
BOARDIND	0.901995	1.875199	0.481013	0.6312

Effects Specification

Period fixed (dummy variables)

R-squared	0.233670	Mean dependent var	146.4444
Adjusted R-squared	0.164897	S.D. dependent var	27.41492
S.E. of regression	25.05284	Akaike info criterion	9.363482
Sum squared resid	97912.57	Schwarz criterion	9.639067
Log likelihood	-785.5777	Hannan-Quinn criter.	9.475303
F-statistic	3.397697	Durbin-Watson stat	1.651911
Prob(F-statistic)	0.000084		

Dependent Variable: DISINDEX
Method: Panel Least Squares
Date: 10/02/14 Time: 17:14
Sample: 2005 2013
Periods included: 9
Cross-sections included: 20
Total panel (unbalanced) observations: 171

Variable	Coefficient	Std. Error	t-Statistic	Prob.
C	117.1817	15.35340	7.632296	0.0000
TASSETS	1.02E-09	5.40E-10	2.186278	0.0313
AGE	1.230592	0.549939	2.237689	0.0268
PAT	2.51E-11	9.32E-11	0.268938	0.7884
FINEXP	0.224094	0.476851	0.469947	0.6391
INTSUB	2.977129	11.76467	0.253057	0.8006
BOARDIND	0.308095	1.115742	0.276134	0.7828

Effects Specification

Cross-section fixed (dummy variables)

R-squared	0.759376	Mean dependent var	146.4444
Adjusted R-squared	0.717889	S.D. dependent var	27.41492
S.E. of regression	14.56119	Akaike info criterion	8.333760
Sum squared resid	30744.08	Schwarz criterion	8.811440
Log likelihood	-686.5365	Hannan-Quinn criter.	8.527582
F-statistic	18.30401	Durbin-Watson stat	2.027834
Prob(F-statistic)	0.000000		

HYPOTHESIS TESTING

Dependent Variable: DISINDEX
Method: Panel Least Squares
Date: 10/02/14 Time: 21:37
Sample: 2005 2013
Periods included: 9
Cross-sections included: 20
Total panel (balanced) observations: 180

Variable	Coefficient	Std. Error	t-Statistic	Prob.
C	145.4137	2.239121	64.94231	0.0000
TASSETS	1.19E-09	5.84E-10	2.038271	0.0430

R-squared	0.022808	Mean dependent var	147.2500
Adjusted R-squared	0.017318	S.D. dependent var	27.74341
S.E. of regression	27.50213	Akaike info criterion	9.477453
Sum squared resid	134633.4	Schwarz criterion	9.512930
Log likelihood	-850.9708	Hannan-Quinn criter.	9.491838
F-statistic	4.154550	Durbin-Watson stat	2.362336
Prob(F-statistic)	0.043002		

Dependent Variable: DISINDEX
Method: Panel Least Squares
Date: 10/02/14 Time: 21:38
Sample: 2005 2013
Periods included: 9
Cross-sections included: 20
Total panel (balanced) observations: 180

Variable	Coefficient	Std. Error	t-Statistic	Prob.
C	148.2501	3.291108	45.04566	0.0000
AGE	0.030104	0.076947	0.391225	0.6961

R-squared	0.000859	Mean dependent var	147.2500
Adjusted R-squared	-0.004754	S.D. dependent var	27.74341
S.E. of regression	27.80928	Akaike info criterion	9.499666
Sum squared resid	137657.4	Schwarz criterion	9.535143
Log likelihood	-852.9699	Hannan-Quinn criter.	9.514050
F-statistic	0.153057	Durbin-Watson stat	2.380726
Prob(F-statistic)	0.696099		

Dependent Variable: DISINDEX
Method: Panel Least Squares
Date: 10/02/14 Time: 21:39
Sample: 2005 2013
Periods included: 9
Cross-sections included: 20
Total panel (unbalanced) observations: 178

Variable	Coefficient	Std. Error	t-Statistic	Prob.
C	148.1793	2.064968	71.75865	0.0000
PAT	4.01E-10	1.31E-10	3.055394	0.0026

R-squared	0.050370	Mean dependent var	146.7022
Adjusted R-squared	0.044975	S.D. dependent var	27.40791
S.E. of regression	26.78448	Akaike info criterion	9.424695
Sum squared resid	126263.9	Schwarz criterion	9.460445
Log likelihood	-836.7978	Hannan-Quinn criter.	9.439193
F-statistic	9.335432	Durbin-Watson stat	1.578210
Prob(F-statistic)	0.002598		

Dependent Variable: VOLDISC
Method: Panel Least Squares
Date: 10/02/14 Time: 17:50
Sample: 2005 2013
Periods included: 9
Cross-sections included: 20
Total panel (unbalanced) observations: 174

Variable	Coefficient	Std. Error	t-Statistic	Prob.
C	51.05536	1.349654	37.82847	0.0000
TASSETS	4.92E-10	1.82E-10	2.707372	0.0075
AGE	0.009421	0.045122	0.208781	0.8349
PAT	8.81E-11	4.15E-11	2.123804	0.0352
FINEXP	0.059185	0.040723	1.453367	0.1480
INTSUB	6.386289	1.390264	4.593579	0.0000

R-squared	0.221752	Mean dependent var	48.86973
Adjusted R-squared	0.198590	S.D. dependent var	9.142820
S.E. of regression	8.184790	Akaike info criterion	7.076306
Sum squared resid	11254.45	Schwarz criterion	7.185239
Log likelihood	-609.6387	Hannan-Quinn criter.	7.120496
F-statistic	9.573900	Durbin-Watson stat	0.434955
Prob(F-statistic)	0.000000		

Dependent Variable: DISINDEX
Method: Panel Least Squares
Date: 10/02/14 Time: 21:39
Sample: 2005 2013
Periods included: 9
Cross-sections included: 20
Total panel (unbalanced) observations: 174

Variable	Coefficient	Std. Error	t-Statistic	Prob.
C	141.7816	2.523606	56.18216	0.0000
FINEXP	0.378036	0.117858	3.207550	0.0016

R-squared	0.056440	Mean dependent var	146.6092
Adjusted R-squared	0.050954	S.D. dependent var	27.42846
S.E. of regression	26.72052	Akaike info criterion	9.420169
Sum squared resid	122805.7	Schwarz criterion	9.456480
Log likelihood	-817.5547	Hannan-Quinn criter.	9.434899
F-statistic	10.28838	Durbin-Watson stat	2.357405
Prob(F-statistic)	0.001597		

Test for Equality of Means Between Series
Date: 10/02/14 Time: 21:49
Sample: 2005 2013
Included observations: 180

Method	df	Value	Probability
Anova F-test	(6, 1242)	10.12697	0.0000
Welch F-test*	(6, 496.21)	898.1744	0.0000

*Test allows for unequal cell variances

Analysis of Variance

Source of Variation	df	Sum of Sq.	Mean Sq.
Between	6	2.15E+21	3.58E+20
Within	1242	4.39E+22	3.53E+19
Total	1248	4.60E+22	3.69E+19

Category Statistics

Variable	Count	Mean	Std. Dev.	Std. Err. of Mean
DISINDEX	180	147.2500	27.74341	2.067872
TASSETS	180	1.54E+09	3.52E+09	2.62E+08
AGE	180	33.22222	27.01284	2.013418
PAT	178	3.68E+09	1.53E+10	1.15E+09
FINEXP	174	12.77011	17.23701	1.306734
INTSUB	180	0.583333	0.494382	0.036849
BOARDIND	177	0.814878	1.077509	0.080991
All	1249	7.47E+08	6.07E+09	1.72E+08

Dependent Variable: DISINDEX
Method: Panel Least Squares
Date: 10/02/14 Time: 21:40
Sample: 2005 2013
Periods included: 9
Cross-sections included: 20
Total panel (balanced) observations: 180

Variable	Coefficient	Std. Error	t-Statistic	Prob.
C	158.3333	3.022785	52.37995	0.0000
INTSUB	19.00000	3.957754	4.800702	0.0000

R-squared	0.114634	Mean dependent var	147.2500
Adjusted R-squared	0.109660	S.D. dependent var	27.74341
S.E. of regression	26.17809	Akaike info criterion	9.378771
Sum squared resid	121982.0	Schwarz criterion	9.414249
Log likelihood	-842.0894	Hannan-Quinn criter.	9.393156
F-statistic	23.04674	Durbin-Watson stat	2.398575
Prob(F-statistic)	0.000003		

Dependent Variable: DISINDEX
Method: Panel Least Squares
Date: 10/02/14 Time: 21:40
Sample: 2005 2013
Periods included: 9
Cross-sections included: 20
Total panel (unbalanced) observations: 177

Variable	Coefficient	Std. Error	t-Statistic	Prob.
C	144.2254	2.599519	55.48158	0.0000
BOARDIND	3.529736	1.927690	1.831070	0.0688

R-squared	0.018799	Mean dependent var	147.1017
Adjusted R-squared	0.013192	S.D. dependent var	27.73947
S.E. of regression	27.55589	Akaike info criterion	9.481545
Sum squared resid	132882.3	Schwarz criterion	9.517434
Log likelihood	-837.1167	Hannan-Quinn criter.	9.496100
F-statistic	3.352817	Durbin-Watson stat	0.448631
Prob(F-statistic)	0.068791		

Pairwise Granger Causality Tests
Date: 10/02/14 Time: 21:48
Sample: 2005 2013
Lags: 2

Null Hypothesis:	Obs	F-Statistic	Prob.
TASSETS does not Granger Cause DISINDEX	140	1.11526	0.3308
DISINDEX does not Granger Cause TASSETS		0.38522	0.6810
AGE does not Granger Cause DISINDEX	140	1.32750	0.2686
DISINDEX does not Granger Cause AGE		0.45383	0.6362
PAT does not Granger Cause DISINDEX	137	0.71476	0.4912
DISINDEX does not Granger Cause PAT		1.71092	0.1847
FINEXP does not Granger Cause DISINDEX	134	0.87992	0.4173
DISINDEX does not Granger Cause FINEXP		0.38209	0.6832
INTSUB does not Granger Cause DISINDEX	140	2.23907	0.1105
DISINDEX does not Granger Cause INTSUB		0.00495	0.9951
BOARDIND does not Granger Cause DISINDEX	133	2.10537	0.1260
DISINDEX does not Granger Cause BOARDIND		1.45968	0.2362
AGE does not Granger Cause TASSETS	140	0.08984	0.9141
TASSETS does not Granger Cause AGE		0.15370	0.8577
PAT does not Granger Cause TASSETS	137	0.38818	0.6791
TASSETS does not Granger Cause PAT		0.08528	0.9183
FINEXP does not Granger Cause TASSETS	134	2.82384	0.0631
TASSETS does not Granger Cause FINEXP		1.22607	0.2968
INTSUB does not Granger Cause TASSETS	140	0.22738	0.7969
TASSETS does not Granger Cause INTSUB		0.19322	0.8245
BOARDIND does not Granger Cause TASSETS	133	0.15914	0.8530
TASSETS does not Granger Cause BOARDIND		0.31478	0.7305

PAT does not Granger Cause AGE	137	11.6545	2.E-05
AGE does not Granger Cause PAT		1.79700	0.1698
FINEXP does not Granger Cause AGE	134	0.14600	0.8643
AGE does not Granger Cause FINEXP		0.11642	0.8902
INTSUB does not Granger Cause AGE	140	0.07973	0.9234
AGE does not Granger Cause INTSUB		0.14465	0.8655
BOARDIND does not Granger Cause AGE	133	0.03211	0.9684
AGE does not Granger Cause BOARDIND		0.24786	0.7808
FINEXP does not Granger Cause PAT	134	0.42892	0.6521
PAT does not Granger Cause FINEXP		2.63512	0.0756
INTSUB does not Granger Cause PAT	137	2.01788	0.1370
PAT does not Granger Cause INTSUB		27.2881	1.E-10
BOARDIND does not Granger Cause PAT	130	0.06548	0.9366
PAT does not Granger Cause BOARDIND		0.18199	0.8338
INTSUB does not Granger Cause FINEXP	134	0.83597	0.4358
FINEXP does not Granger Cause INTSUB		0.03924	0.9615
BOARDIND does not Granger Cause FINEXP	127	0.33231	0.7179
FINEXP does not Granger Cause BOARDIND		6.43927	0.0022
BOARDIND does not Granger Cause INTSUB	133	0.07466	0.9281
INTSUB does not Granger Cause BOARDIND		5.00130	0.0081

INDEX

www.ingramcontent.com/pod-product-compliance
Lightning Source LLC
Chambersburg PA
CBHW030747180526
45163CB00003B/938